Monstrous Possibility

Monstrous

Possibility

An Invitation to Literary Politics

by Curtis White

Dalkey Archive Press | 回

Library of Congress Cataloging-in-Publication Data:

White, Curtis, 1951-
        Monstrous possibility : an invitation to literary politics / by
Curtis White. — 1st ed.
                p.   cm.
        ISBN 1-56478-190-9 (alk. paper)
        1. Postmodernism (Literature) 2. Fiction—20th century—
History and criticism. I. Title.
PN98.P67W45   1998
801'.95'0973—dc21   97-51439
                                                        CIP

This publication is partially supported by a grant from the Illinois
Arts Council, a state agency.

Dalkey Archive Press
Illinois State University
Campus Box 4241
Normal, IL 61790-4241

Printed on permanent/durable acid-free paper and bound in the
United States of America.

contents

Italo Calvino and What's Next:
The Literature of Monstrous Possibility

I'd like to talk about Italo Calvino—particularly his two science fictive books of stories, *Cosmicomics* and *t zero*—within the context of a more general discussion of postmodernism and John Barth's idea of "the literature of exhaustion." I will begin by rectifying the almost universal misunderstanding of "the literature of exhaustion" (as another sign of the death of the novel), but, fortunately, Barth's own later essay, "The Literature of Replenishment," has already unambiguously set things straight. It is enough to say that Barth's first essay, "The Literature of Exhaustion," was not a gloomy prophecy of the end of the novel, or fiction, or print. Rather, both it and "The Literature of Replenishment" are about a single, happier question: what is postmodernism (the "what's next?" of American fiction for the last fifteen to twenty years)?

As a contribution to Barth's discussion of postmodernism, I would like to develop two metaphors, one recent bit of literary theory, and one more or less rhapsodic allusion to an "eternal verity," the human heart, love. My purpose for these fragments will not be to tell the Truth about postmodernism (no doubt an impossible, in any case an undesirable task), but, more modestly, to provide new ways of talking about and looking at it, which—when added to what has already been said about postmodernism, and what remains to be said in the next few decades—will eventually constitute postmodernism's saturation, used-upness, and exhaustion. In short, this is to be a contribution to the death of what's next.

Before setting out, I want to emphasize that I have, as Chuck Berry sang, "No particular place to go." I have no particular understanding or definition for which to claim privilege. Postmodernism is usually defined through a series of literary historical "sightings." Barth catches a glimpse of it in Borges, Nabokov and Beckett. Alan Wilde sees it in Robert Coover, Ronald Sukenick and Raymond Federman. Federman, with greater depth of perception, sees it as far back as Rabelais, and then in Céline and Beckett. The perhaps myopic Jerome Klinkowitz can make it out only in the procreative vortex of 1967 in which Barthelme, Vonnegut and Kosinski came on the scene. Or postmodernism is defined as a trans-traditional itinerary; one gets to it, through Rabelais, Sterne, Joyce, and Gilbert Sorrentino, in the same way that one gets to San Jose through San Mateo and Palo Alto. This is a way of saying what Nietzsche says in *The Genealogy of Morals:* "that which has a history eludes definition." Postmodernism has no definition as such, and like all other literary classifications, it has no pure examples. Its only reality is in a system of equivalences and differences. It is like Joyce and unlike James. Like Sorrentino and unlike Saul Bellow. This ought to mean that postmodernism is nothing in itself, but only whatever we say it is. That is, in fact, what I mean. For, as the aesthetician Morris Weitz has argued, art is what we as a culture decide it is. Postmodernism, too, will be what we decide it will be, or perhaps it will be what writers will need it to be.

The most I intend to do is to hold a certain kind of mirror (what we are used to calling literary commentary) up to the texts that we are used to calling postmodern and hope that there is recognition. Although we may not be able to claim that this recognition is what we used fondly to refer to as knowledge, it is much more than nothing. It is a lively, a bracing, and—above all else—a practical tautology. As the later Wittgenstein of *Philosophical Investigations* would have argued here, the idea of postmodernism may not constitute a truth, but that doesn't make it any less useful. We can still use it even if we do not claim for it any truth. It can still be a tool. This is to say nothing more than what Barth says in "The Literature of Replenishment," that "critical categories are as more or less fishy as they are less or more useful."

As I have already suggested, the writers of the fiction of postmodernism are not so much interested in, or overwhelmed by the idea of exhaustion, as they are excited by other possibilities, by what is not yet tedious. In fact, contemporary fiction is a literature of great promise, productivity, and possibility. It is a literature of monstrous possibility. In Italo Calvino one may find an indication of, as well as a metaphor for, this largeness of possibility in two key related tropes: the *regressus in infinitum,* and the figure of the "monster."

The wobbly history of the notion of the *regressus in infinitum* is a crucial and indicative one for western culture. We may trace it as far back as Zeno, where it is the paradox of Achilles and the tortoise in which movement is proven impossible, for the moving object (Achilles) must run half of the distance before reaching its destination, and before reaching the half, half of the half, and before half of the half, half of the half of the half, and so on. Zeno sought through his paradox to discover the contradiction which inheres in the ordinary idea of motion.

Recently, the significance of the *regressus* (as paradox and critique of the conventional) has again asserted itself, this time, most notably, in the thinking of Jacques Derrida. It is the *regressus in infinitum,* the hopelessness of arriving at an ultimate term, that Derrida applies "deconstructively" to the desire of phenomenology to determine a "transcendental subject." As Husserl (whom Derrida critiques at great length in *Speech and Phenomena*) peels back the layers of consciousness which wrap themselves tightly about the Cartesian cogito, the causal structure of the *regressus in infinitum* is—at a crucial point—broken, ruptured by metaphysics, theology, and desire. Husserl was determined to find a privileged, originary break in the chain of causality which he called the *I,* the cogito, His Majesty the Sovereign Self. Derrida's modest but deconstructing reminder to all of metaphysics is that, after all, the *regressus* is the name of a paradox (of an "undecidability"), and not, as Saint Thomas Aquinas, Descartes or Husserl would have it, of a theological, metaphysical or phenomenological proof.

Italo Calvino uses the metaphor of the *regressus in infinitum* in his cosmicomical story "A Sign in Space." In it he finds the idea of the origin of language caught within the dialectical structure of the *regressus.* The results for his narrator, Qfwfq, and language itself are both bizarre and comic: "I conceived the idea of making a sign, that's true enough, or rather, I conceived the idea of considering a

9

sign a something that I felt like making, so when, at that point in space and not in another, I made something, meaning to make a sign, it turned out that I really had made a sign, after all . . ." Here Calvino wraps himself in the contradictoriness of language trying to deliver the facts about its own origin. How conceive, how make, how feel? What something, what point, what meaning could there be before the first sign? Calvino asserts, comically, the undecidability, the utter perplexity of the question of the origin of signs, for the existence of a sign is dependent on the assumption of the existence of other signs before it. There is always already an earlier sign:

> I thought about it day and night; in fact, I couldn't think about anything else; actually, this was the first opportunity I had had to think something; or I should say: to think something had never been possible, first because there were no things to think about, and second because signs to think of them by were lacking, but from the moment there was that sign, it was possible for someone thinking to think of a sign, and therefore that one, in the sense that the sign was the thing you could think about and also the sign of the thing thought, namely, itself.

If it is true that the history of all Western thought is the history of the fate of a handful of metaphors, the present stature of the *regressus in infinitum,* once again—as in Zeno—a deconstructing paradox, is instructive. Through the *regressus,* an important part of literary postmodernism (certainly Borges, Calvino and Barth, all rooted in Nietzsche and Kafka) seems to be saying, in Borges's words in *Labyrinths,* "We . . . have dreamt the world. We have dreamt it as firm, mysterious, visible, ubiquitous in space and durable in time; but in its architecture we have allowed tenuous and eternal crevices of unreason which tell us it is false."

If, couched in our postmodern period, we may not speak of origins or dream the world as "ubiquitous in space and durable in time" without tainting ourselves with theology and metaphysics, how shall we explain the "presence" of things (you know: chairs, streets, people, bad manners) in our stories? What shall we say about them? The ultimate thrust of the deconstructions of Zeno, Derrida, Borges and Calvino is to cut us off from time, space and matter, that is to say, from the mimetic impulse. But what sort of reality can fiction have, deprived of all claim to referentiality?

One may discern in Calvino two related responses to this question. The first, arrived at, again, in the story "A Sign in Space," is that the only reality the cosmos has is the reality of signs. The sign which Calvino's Qfwfq created "inhabited me, possessed me entirely, came between me and everything with which I might have attempted to establish a relationship." As the story concludes even more forcefully, "independent of signs, space didn't exist and perhaps had never existed."

Although this is a lot, this isn't all Calvino has to say on the question of presence. What about, for example, the presence of birds? Calvino begins his short story "The Origin of the Birds" (*t zero*) with Qfwfq saying that in order to tell the story of the origin of birds he would have to "remember better how a number of things were made, things I've long since forgotten; first the thing I now call bird, second what I now call I, third the branch, fourth the place where I was looking out, fifth all the others." In the place of what Qfwfq had "long since forgotten" (origins: how things were made), Calvino supplies the figure of the monster, "all those who could exist and didn't." Qfwfq tells the story this way:

> One morning I hear some singing, outside, that I have never heard before. Or rather (since we didn't yet know what singing was), I hear something making a sound that nobody has ever made before. I look out. I see an unknown animal singing on a branch. He had wings feet tail claws spurs feathers plumes fins quills beak teeth crop horns crest wattles and a star on his forehead. It was a bird; you've realized that already, but I didn't, they had never been seen before . . .

The appearance of the bird is profoundly unsettling for Qfwfq and his community. The wisest among them, old U(h), speaks to his neighbors in the name of tradition. " 'Don't look at him' he says. 'He's a mistake.' " But Qfwfq takes a more difficult and risky line:

Hadn't we been told over and over that everything capable of being born from the Reptiles had been born? . . . For many years we had been tormented by doubts as to who was a monster and who wasn't, but that too could be considered long settled: all of us who existed were nonmonsters, while the monsters were all those who could exist and didn't. . . . But if we were going to begin again with strange animals, . . . if a creature impossible by definition such as a bird was instead possible . . . then the barrier between monsters and nonmonsters was exploded and everything was possible again.

What I would like to suggest is that this idea of a presence grounded, not in original birdiness, but rather in a monstrous and disruptive paste-up of mutative reptile and fish is not only an important philosophical idea (because it implicitly denies a metaphysical/ theological origin), but a crucial literary distinction as well. For there is a monstrous figure in the carpet here: the story is told through descriptions of comic-strip frames. Calvino as author, as much as Qfwfq as character, is, as Calvino says in his essay "Myth in the Narrative," "the promoter of a process of refusal to see and say things the way they had been seen and said up to that very moment."

The literature of postmodernism generally aspires to origin as rupture, break, mutation, and transformation. It prefers the discontinuous and the monstrous to the linear and archetypal. Consider, for example, that there is no possibility for the monstrous in Northrop Frye's mythopoeic literary universe. In that cosmos literature's lineage is proper—Hamlet rooted in ur-Hamlets rooted in universal myth—and its papers and credentials are in order. But from Rabelais's gargantuan, encyclopaedic farce, through Fielding's comic epic poem in prose, Sterne's autobiography in utero, Joyce's comic catalogues, Federman's exaggerated secondhand tale to be read aloud either standing or sitting, Barth's "Fiction for Print, Tape and Live Voice," and, surely the most appropriate example of all, Barth's triptych, *Chimera,* the inclination of the postmodern, which is to say of the antimimetic, has been for the hybrid, for the a-generic. Of course, these monstrous genres are meant to show that the norms defining monstrosity are themselves "originally" monstrous. This is precisely the shock of Qfwfq's insight; the line has been crossed; we are all monsters.

However, aside from the undecidable question of the original constitution of parts, Calvino's monsters, whether biological or literary, are always recognizable in their parts. It is never a question of creation from nothing, but only of newness as a recombination of previously existing parts. Calvino sees the creation of narrative as "a combinatorial game which plays on the possibilities intrinsic to its own material."

This seems to me to be an important theoretical assertion. It is to say that the storyteller is not Shakespeare's old mimeser (with his mirror held to nature), nor even, in any simple sense, Joyce's old artificer (that high priest to the Imagination), but rather something much more like Claude Levi-Strauss's *bricoleur*. In the chapter "The Science of the Concrete" in his book *The Savage Mind,* Levi-Strauss defines the *bricoleur* as one whose "universe of instruments is closed" and who must "make do with whatever is at hand." The *bricoleur* is "imprisoned in the events and experiences which he never tires of ordering and re-ordering in his search to find them a meaning."

So, the monstrousness of postmodernism's literary possibilities is the result, on the one hand, of the debunking or deconstructing of certain central conventions of nineteenth-century literary realism, especially of the notions of mimesis and genre, and, on the other hand, of the willingness to allow narrative's newly released parts to float, mingle and re-cohere. The realist values the reassurance of the familiar; the excitable postmodernist—a curious *bricoleur*—values the beauty of the new and monstrous. As Qfwfq would say, "the barrier between monsters and nonmonsters is exploded and everything is possible again."

As relevant as the *regressus in infinitum* and the figures of the monster and the *bricoleur* seem to what is central in Calvino's fiction and in postmodernism in general, one is forced to admit that most of Calvino's tales of Qfwfq in *Cosmicomics* and *t zero* are, from a certain perspective, preeminently recognizable, hardly monstrous tales of love, loneliness and philosophical gloom and glee. Calvino is clearly one who manages, as John Barth writes, "to speak eloquently and memorably to our still-human hearts and conditions, as the great artists have always done." But what does Barth mean by our "still-human hearts and conditions"? Is it true of Calvino? And if it is, how does it work with what we have to this point characterized as postmodern?

It seems to me that just beneath the surface of the modernist-postmodernist tradition, just under its icy theoretical and structural speculations, just beyond its often acid criticism of the bourgeois, is a stratum of a certain kind of sentimentality. Consider, briefly, Proust's *Swann's Way*.

Proust's official attitude towards "representation" is something like "one never gets to put down the book." In the opening passage of *Swann's Way,* the narrator has been reading, has put down his book, has slept, dreamt and become the subject of his book, and then awoke to try to put down the book once more. Consciousness is textual, for Proust, and reality is the supplementary "structure of recollection." A place is real for the narrating Marcel only if one has heard or read about it beforehand and had time to imagine and dream about its particular character.

In the same way, Swann's love was nothing in itself, but existed only to the extent that he could base it upon his own "sound, aesthetic foundation." The truth of his love is, as the narrator points out repeatedly, composed not so much by a person, Swann's lover, Odette, as by "a face deserving to be found in Botticelli" and a phrase of music.

Even one's experiences and emotions (that is, one's subjectivity) are authored by outside others. For even though the narrator authors Swann's story, Swann's experiences are more importantly the author of the narrator's own experiences in love. For the narrator would never have had his feelings for Gilberte (who was also "authored" by Swann) if he hadn't known of Swann's feelings for and experiences with Odette. He is that distinguished French person—descendent of Stendahl's Julian Sorel and Flaubert's Emma Bovary—who never would have fallen in love if he hadn't read about it first.

And yet in spite of Marcel's lucid speculations on the supple-

1 4

mental and textual nature of all experience—especially the romantic—love and beauty, as they take their places in his life, are overwhelming. In short, the presence of romantic love in Proust's fiction is so central and powerful that theory seems ultimately inconsequent: all that we know not to be—is utterly real.

Much the same sort of contradictory impulse exists in Calvino. Alongside his rigorous passages on the nature of the cosmos as the realm of signs, there is an attitude towards love/sex as a chemical/organic foundation, as an originary disposition of living matter or cells (much like, perhaps, John Barth's sperm cells in "Night Sea Journey" that launch themselves into the unknown with the cry of "Love! Love! Love!"). Take, for example, this passage from the story "The Distance of the Moon" in *Cosmicomics*. Qfwfq is trying to overcome the attraction of the moon—which, in this story, hangs at only a distance of yards from the earth:

> "Hold on! Hold on to us!" they shouted at me, and in all that groping, sometimes I ended up by seizing one of Mrs. Vhd Vhd's breasts, which were round and firm, and the contact was good and secure and had an attraction as strong as the Moon's or even stronger, especially if I managed,as I plunged down, to put my other arm around her hips, and with this I passed back into our world . . .

Thus, Calvino's cosmic character settles on the breast of the lover, in the breast of the mother, in the breast of nature, in the breast of the cosmos.

Most of Calvino's stories are about either the change caused by biological evolution or the change caused by distancing (the gradual or exploding expansion of the universe). Evolution from a happy original state when, as in the story "Blood, Sea" *(t zero)*, we were present in the sea and the sea was present in us; and expansion in the cosmos to the point where the galaxies are "gradually reduced to the last tail of the last luminous ray," become metaphors for loneliness which create, in turn, a powerful nostalgia for lost origins.

In "The Spiral," a story about the social life of a mollusc, we glimpse this radiant origin:

I knew that some of the others were female. The water transmitted a special vibration, a kind of brrrum brrrum brrrum, I remember when I became aware of it the first time, or rather, not the first, I remember when I became aware of being aware of it as a thing I had always known. At the discovery of these vibrations' existence, I was seized with a great curiosity, not so much to see them, or to be seen by them either . . . but a curiosity to know whether something would happen between me and them. A desperation filled me, a desire not to do anything special, which would have been out of place, knowing that there was nothing special to do, or nonspecial either, but to respond in some way to that vibration with a corresponding vibration, or rather, with a personal vibration of my own, because, sure enough, there was something there that wasn't exactly the same as the other, I mean now you might say it came from hormones, but for me it was very beautiful. . . . In other words, I had fallen in love.

This caring or this nostalgia, this sentiment or this generosity, this desire to spare love from what is otherwise a thorough and materialist critique of certain philosophies, myths and romances that have dominated our literature and culture since the nineteenth century and before, this, too, is a prominent part of both modernism and postmodernism. It can he found in Molly Bloom's universal "yes," in the helping touch of the hands of "the ladies" in Kafka's "The Hunger Artist," in Humbert Humbert's rhapsodic, albeit glandular, desires, negatively in any number of Donald Barthelme's "sad" stories (like "Critique de la Vie Quotidienne"), and in the tireless love of Lady Amherst and Ambrose Mensch in John Barth's *Letters*. "Love" is, perhaps, that baby in the bathwater of realism that much postmodernism does not for the moment care, or dare, to throw out. Without it there is only that terrifying loneliness that, as Wallace Stevens put it, is "nothing to have at heart."

I would like finally to retreat a step in my argument in order to say that postmodernism, even though it values and uses the figure of the monster, is no recent disruption or monster itself (except perhaps as an eternally recurring monster). Postmodernism is the locus of a "crisis of language" (Roland Barthes) that is at least as old as Rabelais and, if we knew where to look for it, certainly older. It is, simply, a part of the Other Tradition of antimimesis, that much vilified and unholy mirror reflection of F. R. Leavis's Great Tradition. Now, this would be no great thing, and postmodernism could make for itself no claim for great or surprising profundity, except for the fact that the relationship between the two has been highly charged with cultural, ideological, and political values. The need to react against the orthodoxy of realism is more than what John Barth contends, that is, it is more than a simple matter of the exhaustion of nineteenth century and modernist modes. For the confrontation between realism and "experimentalism" is not only a narrow, provincial, literary dispute, it is also part of a broader ideological battle between not necessarily but factually combative epistemologies. Realism has become a State Fiction, a part of the machinery of the political state. It is through the conventions of Realism that the State explains to its citizens the relationship between themselves and Nature, economics, politics, and their own sexuality. This massive epistemological exercise takes place every day, right before our eyes on television, in the movies, in *Time* magazine, in the simpleminded, causal rhetoric of politicians, and so on. What postmodernism has done and continues to do is oppose any totalizing fiction of life, that which, in Calvino's words, seeks "to confirm and consecrate the established order of things."

Of course, ideally the two sides could live peacefully. The fact of the matter is that they cannot live separately, although that fact can be occluded or denied for political reasons. The mimetic needs the antimimetic if it is not to become redundant and authoritarian; it needs the consciousness and the good conscience of its own ultimately fictive base, which the antimimetic provides. Likewise, the antimimetic needs to be aware that it is always at some level part of what it critiques. It needs the as-if of referentiality unless it desires to break down into "writing at the zero degree," or "white writing," or the Writerly, or any other dream text of the avant-garde, the only knowledge of which we have is that, as Barthes says, there are no examples of it. This is to say that no texts are mimetic and that, nevertheless, all texts must behave, at some level, as if they were. In short, mimesis and antimimesis, realism and experimentalism are oppositions that exist only through an exercise of force, and which, therefore, tell us as much about the politics of our own time as they do about language or literature.

And so, finally, Calvino is an exemplary postmodernist not only because he is one of those few people whose artistic thinking is as hip as any French novelist's, but because he manages nonetheless to speak to "our still-human hearts and conditions," but also because, as Barth does not seem to consider, Calvino sees the confrontation between modernism- postmodernism and realism not as a narrowly literary dispute, but rather as an important part of a much larger cultural confrontation over the frontiers of knowledge and power. This overtly political aim is implicit in his fiction, implicit particularly in the way his play with scientific fact disrupts our conventional understanding of the world. But Calvino is explicit in his essay "Myth in the Narrative":

> When written literature comes into being, it already bears the burden of the duty to confirm and consecrate the established order of things, a burden from which it slowly frees itself . . . in order to express the very oppressions it labors beneath, to bring them to full consciousness and to transmit this consciousness to the culture and thought of a whole society.

1984

A Literature in Opposition:
Reconstructing the Future

1

There is a coherence, a vitality, and a purpose to recent American fiction that make it—where it is enlarging its capacities and comprehensiveness—a literature in opposition. What is crucial and unique about this most recent fiction is its alliance with critical theory. I would like to propose a probable logic of events for American fiction of the last two decades. I mean by *probable logic* approximately what the Italian theorist Antonio Negri means by *tendency*. The "tendency," for Negri, "is above all what permits a reading of the present in light of the future, in order to make projects to illuminate the future." Postmodernist fiction's acts of radical imagination, poststructuralism's corroboration of a postmodern critique of Realism, a subsequent rereading of Marx and Western Marxism: these are the terms of a decisive assertion of the political within contemporary American literature.

Of course, there have been vigorous denials of such claims for the contemporary avant-garde's social relevance. Most conspicuously, in the 1970s, there was the Moral Fiction reaction begun by John Gardner and given institutional credibility by Gerald Graff *(Literature against Itself)* and Reginald Gibbons (editor of *Tri-Quarterly*) at Northwestern University.

The politics of the American literary disruption called postmodernism have always been ambiguous. Even though writers like John Barth, Kurt Vonnegut, John Hawkes, Donald Barthelme, and Richard Brautigan got their foothold within the official literary canon during the ascendancy of the "counterculture" of the sixties, and their readers were the "right" people politically (unlike the Right people who read Bellow, Updike, Malamud, and Cheever), there was always something frustrating and incomplete about the relationship between their radical acts of imagination and coherent politics. For instance, there was a general reluctance among the best-known postmodernists to align themselves with leftism. Some, like William Gass, were aggressively apolitical, even when faced with the plainly ideological attack of Moral Fiction in the late seventies, as Gass was during several well-known debates with John Gardner. Others self-consciously drew the line of their politics well short of leftism, as Barth did with his notion of "tragic viewing liberalism."

The situation was not clarified by postmodernism's early critics. Ihab Hassan was metaphysical and unrelentingly academic; Jerome Klinkowitz plainly aspired to some sort of radicalism, but his thinking was so fuzzy that his work ultimately amounted to little more than a sort of literary Greening of America: a high-octane pep talk for the avant-garde, but running on empty as theory. In general, the vast majority of critics and scholars have been studiously apolitical in their estimations of the worth of American "experimentalism." It has been proper to ask whether postmodernism's art is better or worse than other kinds of art (especially mimetic art), but not what its relationship as marginal literary discourse is to a dominant literary discourse.

Whatever the shortcomings of postmodernism's theory and politics, however frail its grasp upon its own situation, it has never failed to feel itself involved in an antagonism of some sort. The terms of that antagonism have rarely been allowed to extend beyond the limits of an aesthetic enmity with the Great Tradition of Anglo-American Realism. If American experimental writers understood anything at the heart of the heart of their Otherness, it was simply that they had a right to their difference, to their way of writing stories and seeing the world.

But, as with American modernism, there was something about this pluralism, this cussedness in the face of the totalizing, that remained, in Hugh Kenner's phrase, "homemade." It was sense of "right" that didn't know how to transcend its American liberal

2 0

democratic origins. In short, much of the theoretical and political naivete of the 1960s counterculture, what Herbert Marcuse despaired of ever becoming a real opposition to "administered society," was also true of the counterculture's favorite fiction writers, the authors of *Cat's Cradle, Snow White,* and even the notoriously self-knowing *Sot-Weed Factor.* So the task of describing the political implications of writing at the margins, at the "zero degree," essentially avoided by the canonized writers and their critics, had to be pursued elsewhere, most notably in the work of French critical theorists.

What occurred around 1968, supported by the arrival and "dissemination" of English translations of the works of Jacques Derrida, the poststructural Roland Barthes (especially *S/Z*), and Jacques Lacan, was the decisive and irreversible expansion of American literature—holed up as it had at last come to be in the university—through the continental tradition of linguistic, philosophic, and political theory. For those writers who cared to pay attention (unlike those described by Frank Lentricchia who flaunted "contempt for the critical and scholarly work of their 'unimaginative' colleagues, all the while mainly conforming to the canonical choices and definitions of the Ph.D.s"), what poststructural theory provided, not perhaps for the first time but nonetheless significantly, was thoroughly articulated arguments about the doctrine of representation (the so-called "structure of reference"), about the question of self-identity, whether that be an Ego's or a text's, and about the interplay of literary and political knowledge, that is, about the relationship of ourselves and our beloved crafts to power. Within deconstruction's now crabbed, now fluid, always difficult, yet always quickening books, one could find the essentials of a logic for the political importance of an avant-grade, an Other tradition to all Great Traditions.

Never before had the assumptions behind the Leavisian "study of life," the sunlit virtues of Hemingway's bulls, balls, and trout lovingly packed in layers of ferns, seemed more suspect, perhaps insidious. Realism's claim to the power to make "present" was reduced to the stature of brightly painted lawn figures (well, reduced to "artifice"). It wasn't that one could no longer trot the little creatures out to beguile the neighbors, it was that, as with Flannery

O'Connor's "artificial nigger," there were certain claims that could no longer be made, particularly claims of adequacy to the Natural or the True.

Clearly, what is important to see in this "writerly" appropriation of deconstructive logic is not simply that it liberates writers from *Field and Stream* narrative doxology, but that it implies a critique of ideology, that is, the representation of the world through images that pretend to be natural, adequate, and proper. It is the Derridean insistence on the nonidentity of Identity, the contamination of the Same with what is Other, that provides the insight for this critique.

Needless to say, there are those writers who proceed indifferent to the challenges posed by theory, doing what comes "naturally." But, for those who would use poststructural thought to insist upon the availability of narrative strategies other than Realism, the political implications may not be avoided. The difference between the Great Tradition and its plural Other has been and remains an opposition with necessary political, social, and aesthetic qualities.

The contention that the postmodern and poststructural have a commonality of purpose that includes historical, social, and political engagement has been the object of highly visible criticism. Among these critiques, it is the revisions of former advocates that are most disturbing, particularly that of *Tri-Quarterly* founder Charles Newman's *The Post-Modern Aura—The Act of Fiction in an Age of Inflation,* and theorist turned anti-theorist Stanley Fish's "Consequences." Charles Newman and *Tri-Quarterly* were, of course, enormously influential in establishing the reputation of the first generation of American postmodernists. The subsequent fame of writers like Barth, Robert Coover, and Gass led to the general acknowledgment of *Tri-Quarterly* as the best of the academic literary reviews. If anyone has earned the right to include the autobiographical within a critical estimation of postmodernism, it is Charles Newman. As it turns out, the autobiographical is present in *The Post-Modern Aura,* but it is an odd presence that manifests itself only obliquely, in the intensity of the book's expression, in the extremity of its logic, and in the thoroughness of its recanting of the recent past, a past with which Newman himself was intimately involved.

The argument of *The Post-Modern Aura* is not simple. In fact, while in the thicket of Newman's myriad and often grotesque generalizations and declarations, it is difficult to know that there is an argument at all. Basically, Newman claims that, like the economics of its time, postmodernism suffers from "inflation," a hyperestimation of its influence and purpose: "the false productivity of inflation coextensive with the exaggerated dynamism of art." In particular, Newman is concerned to deny postmodernism's claim to being a literature in opposition and to insist that any careful analysis of contemporary culture and the postmodern's place within it will show postmodernism to be grossly deluded about its real social effects: "The Avant-Garde has lost any sense of historical relation, the solipsistic impulse has frittered away its detachment and pathos, eclecticism has become timid and defensive, and the cutting edge of Nihilistic perplexity is increasingly translated as mere articles of bad faith, spawning only yet another of America's mindless religious revivals." Although Newman attempts to distance himself from the arguments of the moral fictioneers, it is clear that a substantial part of his objections to postmodernism is "moral." He is as willing as John Gardner was to dismiss, with a sneer, the effect of the postmodern. Gardner wrote that Barth, et al. were mere "aesthetic game players . . . juggling, obscenely giggling and gesturing in the wings while the play of life groans on." Newman uses a voice no less hysterical to characterize the postmodern as an attempt "to resurrect the dissipated scandal of Modernism in which a band of outsiders storm the Temple, like a film run backwards to puerile laughter."

What has always bothered me most about the moral fiction position, and what bothers me most about Newman's book, is its tremendous unfairness, that is, inaccuracy. Although Newman may valorize—like F. R. Leavis before him—the idea of a "vivid and intensely personal experience of life," none of that precious rigor is wasted on the writers he studies. What can be done in any seriousness with a depiction of this sort? "Thus Post-Modernism may in fact mean something beyond its more semantically febrile versions of Art post-partum, post-mortem and post-ponable—a nomenclature which inevitably calls to mind a band of vainglorious contemporary artists following the circus elephants of Modernism with snow shovels." Perhaps this is the nastiest, cleverest thing since Pope was reduced to a hunched back, a case of the clap, and a snotty septum, but it is hardly the basis for a serious examination of anything. What is really at stake here, beyond truth and falsity, has much more to do with desire and destination, with that pippin of autobiography at the heart of Newman's project. It is here that one's objections become most serious. For *The Post-Modern Aura*'s willful determination that nothing of postmodernism be allowed to endure as valuable for the future, while understandable as an expression of an anguished conversion for Newman, has undesirable, merely nihilistic consequences for literary culture in general.

In the name of what superior value or practice does Newman encourage us to turn from the postmodern, to consign to a "fire built largely from books" our own most recent work? It would be bad enough if *The Post-Modern Aura* were just another moment in the Brecht-Lukacs debate, another atavistic, mechanistic assertion that "our real enemies remain the old-fashioned, intractable ones: concentrations of economic and political power which have become inflexible." But it is worse for Newman, after reducing postmodernism to dismissible cartoons, to suffer from a failure of nerve, and refuse to recognize what his diagnosis calls for—a return to political literalism. Instead, he concludes limply that an adequate response to our social situation is merely "not that," not postmodernism.

If Newman were more willing to look for differences rather than redundancies between modernism and postmodernism, and if he were willing to consider literature's present relation to social change as integrated but not necessarily in a vanguard, he might arrive at a more balanced, more workable notion of the significance of a contemporary avant-garde. For example, it is important to realize that contemporary writers, unlike their modernist predecessors, suffer from no illusions about the desirability of a willed alienation from their culture. They are in place, on the job. The place of writers within universities (yes, even writing workshops) makes them more than ever a part of the machinery of exchange, value, and exploitation. They are part, as Antonio Negri would say, of the "sociality of money." This seems to me an instance of primary involvement that writers can claim as valuable, and not, as the case has been too often in the past, as a misfortune to be endured, like the vagaries of patronage or the *Saturday Evening Post*. Modest though the position may be, it allows one to say, yes, Charles Newman, the old problems remain the intractable ones, but that includes Flaubert's problems, that is loosening the culture's—especially our students'—hold on such *ideés recues* as the easy opposition of fact to fiction, inside to outside, feeling to thought, democracy to communism. For this, Barth and Barthes are invaluable aids. Simultaneously, this pedagogy for (if not of) the oppressed might work toward the definition of new needs to be expressed (as Michael Ryan argues) as Rights (a right for example not to have to "grow up absurd," as Paul Goodman put it). All of which would result, one might hope, in a greater disinclination for people merely to take their places in administered society.

This is important work. It is a grounding of literary activity in social value. If my perception of the logic of events in American literature is correct, it is an essential part of the purpose of postmodern and poststructural thought. It is to be preferred to Charles Newman's disgust with his own past.

2

Newman's *The Post-Modern Aura* dovetails cleanly with recent revisions in literary theory insofar as Newman sees postmodernism as a "temporary abandonment of traditional American aesthetic pragmatism." Just as Newman encourages postmodernists to submit their own work to the fire, so the recent essays of Stanley Fish, "Consequences," and Steven Knapp and Walter Benn Michaels, "Against Theory," insist that the "whole enterprise of critical theory is misguided and should be abandoned." The argument I will elaborate on is essentially that made by Daniel O'Hara in his response to Knapp and Michaels, that the effect of this work is "nihilistic, and so even in the best possible light . . . aids and comforts the champions of the status quo."

My principal interest is in Fish's "Consequences," but since that essay is first a response to Knapp and Michaels's "Against Theory," a brief description of their argument is necessary. Knapp and Michaels's position is fundamentally that all theory either attempts to attain a privileged position outside any interpretative practice, from which metacritical distance it may "govern interpretations of particular texts," or it denies the possibility of that position. What undermines these two types of theory, for Knapp and Michaels, is their failure to see problems of authorial intention, literary meaning, and the role of interpretation as false problems. The separation of intention from meaning is, as deconstruction would put it, a distinction without a difference. "The meaning of a text is simply identical to the author's intended meaning." The final consequence of this insight, for its authors, is that theory "is the name for all the ways people have tried to stand outside practice in order to govern practice from without. Our thesis has been that no one can reach a position outside practice, that theorists should stop trying, and that the theoretical enterprise should therefore come to an end."

One of the more conspicuous ironies of Knapp and Michaels's essay is that their dismissal of the metaphysics of interpretation through the destruction of the opposition between "intention" and "meaning" evokes the work of Derrida without evoking it. Plainly, the repressed in this text is the anti-ontological theory of deconstruction. In the intensity of their discussion of the hubbub between historical intention and formalist meaning, poststructural thought is left curiously out of the picture. It is forgotten, even though some of its techniques are curiously applied. As Derrida never fails to point out, such forgetting is always purposeful. Reduced to more manageable dimensions, denuded of the riddles of the subject, the relation of knowledge to power, etc., critical practice, in Knapp and Michaels's hands, is at last freed from the anxiety of all self-scrutiny, and returned to the "natural": doing "what everyone always does."

Stanley Fish's response to "Against Theory" begins by correcting the conspicuous absence of "antifoundationalist theory"— theory in the radically skeptical or deconstructive tradition—in Knapp and Michaels's account. Nevertheless, Fish claims an alliance in purpose, agrees that "theory's day is dying," but insists that the reasoning behind this position must be commensurate with the complexity of the beast it would tame. Fish's logic arrives at the following conclusions: (1) A position is a theory if it claims an ontological higher ground to interpretation, but it may not have consequences as theory because, echoing Knapp and Michaels, its "substitution of the general for the local . . . will never succeed simply because the primary data and formal laws necessary to its success will always be spied or picked out from within the contextual circumstances of which they are supposedly independent." In the lingo of deconstruction, "the critique will be found contaminated by the problem"; (2) A position may not be a theory and yet have important consequences in practice if it is the description of "powerful regularities." Works like William Empson's *Seven Types of Ambiguity* fall into this category, but they are examples of "empirical generalization" and not of theory; (3) The final possibility is that a position be theoretical and have consequences, but not theoretical consequences: "There is a world of difference between saying that theory is a form of practice and saying that theory informs practice . . . theory's success, in short, has been largely political." Fish's claim is shrewdly made. Yes, it is true, "antifoundationalist" or poststructural theory has no necessary consequences, "as an inherent property," for interpretative practice. Its consequences are, of course, for those theories and practices that would claim "fundamentalism," or a fundamental grounding in the True. These stand exposed in their plurality, and in their relation to an unconfessed political agenda or purpose—no small consequence in the eyes of some. But the most urgent consequence of the "antifoundational"—which Fish grants, but grants without esteeming—is precisely political. The "antifoundational" has altered our understanding of knowledge and authority within the "discipline," and it has altered what we can practice in good faith when we teach, interpret, or create.

I think it is possible to see at this point in the early declarations of the New Pragmatism's recoil against theory a kind of xenophobia. Our tango of approach to and avoidance of the European tradition in philosophy and literature has been intensifying since the 1930s. The desperate hostility of the New Pragmatists—antitheorists and moral fictioneers alike—is a kind of last-chance appeal to reconsider the alien-among-us. The controversy over the practice of theory in American literature departments is, as Stanley Fish rightly sees, the consequence of "the emigration of European scholars in the late 1930s." It is also important, especially for the humanities, to see that what got chased out of Fascist Germany was precisely

Marxist theorists: Adorno, Horkheimer, Brecht, Benjamin, Fromm, Lowenthal, and Marcuse. And of those continental thinkers of major influence in the sixties and seventies—Derrida, Barthes, Foucault, Lacan, Althusser, and Kristeva—only Derrida's early, "purely" philosophical work (pre-*Positions*) has been without political implications.

This might seem to be an exercise in the obvious, but the consequences for Fish's argument are enormous. His claim is that theory's merely political success is without interest because "the political is what . . . every theorist desires to rise above." This obviously ignores the fact that antifoundational theory's recent interest in literature and interpretation has been part of an interest in cultural production in general, an interest in literature's place in the social. Fish seems to be in a position of saying, along with Knapp and Michaels, let us not do theory if it will not provide us with ultimate grounds; let us do what we've always done, "thematizing," with Milton or whomever else; but above all let us not consider the unseemly theme of valorizing precisely the politics of literary theory. Within "Consequences" that is the one option Fish does not let his acute sense of consequence entertain.

The simple consequence of all I have been discussing, a consequence about which American literature has become increasingly insistent, is that the social world is constructed, does not participate in the necessity of nature, and can be constructed otherwise. Postmodernism has struggled admirably to provide that which a Marxist deconstruction would require: reconstruction. Postmodernism has, following the young Marx of "The German Ideology," attempted "to interpret reality in another way, i.e., to recognize it by another interpretation." Borges, for instance, finding in his meditations on Zeno that our ordinary understandings of space and time are flawed by "tenuous and eternal crevices of unreason." Needless to say, even with a guide as discerning as Borges, one proceeds here skeptically, mindful of the dangers and follies of utopic thinking.

Nevertheless, one of my necessary assumptions has been that we are still residents of a time when meaning, consciousness, negativity—in short, politics as the confrontation of ideologies—are meaningful, and that change is real. But perhaps the opposite is true. Perhaps it is the case that our search for a critical practice based upon desire informed by analysis is simply part of the already moribund history of Western Reason. Perhaps our critical methods really are as irrelevant as they daily seem to the working of the media and the conveyance of icons (that which saturates consciousness without having to be meaningful). Perhaps, as Paul Virilio suggests, the really telling consequences are beyond the ideological, embedded in the superpowers' complicity, in their gruesome mutual dependence on technology accelerated to its ultimate and catastrophic term (see Paul Virilio, *Pure War*).

Always, for our own time, there is the possibility that to answer the question, "What is the space, what are the modalities, for discursive contestation?" is to reply, "That space is no longer in the picture; it is beside the point; your enemy is once again not where he was." The willingness of American culture in particular to allow its subjects a welter of discursive possibilities, the conduction of messages from Joan Collins to the Grundrisse, of no significance in their difference to power, might seem to mean that, as Wallace Stevens wrote, chaos can be a great order. Great and oppressive. The reckoning of orthodoxies may, in these late innings of the game, be unnecessary to the maintenance of power. For, according to Paul Virilio, "Reagan's politics are ahead of the times: you concentrate power on war, on economic and military-industrial development, etc., and you let the rest drop dead. This comes down to saying: 'manage yourselves, do what you want, take care of your own sexual customs, do your thing in life, and we'll take care of the rest.' "

Certainly, postmodernism, or any contemporary culture of resistance, is deluded if it imagines that its effectiveness will be a measure of how successfully it can "lead" the "masses," those whom Jean Baudrillard describes as "the shadow cast by power," their silence "the silence of beasts" (see Jean Baudrillard, *In the Shadow of the Silent Majorities*). But leaving behind that anachronistic ambition does not leave the writer without a project. As I have already argued, contemporary writers are more intensely, more conspicuously situated in the social and economic than they have ever been. Their madness has at last been institutionalized (in universities) and "disciplined" (by their field: creative writing). What I would like to suggest finally—following, again, Antonio Negri—is that we make the specifics of our work place, the place where we receive our wages and enter the "sociality of money," the specifics of our resistance. Here, too, there is plenty of room for delusion, but at the very least we proceed with "animal faith" in the possibility of change, autonomously, and with the integrity of our own well-defined desires. I mean to encourage no one to optimism. The terms of this contest remain what they were for the Frankfurt School, hopelessly unequal. We can participate, for the present, at best merely in a "negative dialectics." For even if the essential logic of the most important recent movements in literary art and theory has been politically leftist, that does little to deny that literary academia is wed to the status quo, has little desire to understand what political power it might claim for itself, and is in fact—as Knapp and Michaels have demonstrated for us—eager to take seriously arguments that reinstitute what one had assumed was a thoroughly discredited philosophy of the literal, the self-evident, and the practical. Here, plainly, academia's pluralism is indistinguishable from self-paralysis.

This is perhaps to say little more than that academics, like other laborers, are still working toward political enlightenment. And even though there is no guarantee of success, it seems to me desirable to attempt—in the meantime—to describe certain alternatives for writers and theorists as teachers. We can refuse to keep to our job description as "purveyors of truth," in Derrida's phrase. We can instead debunk the idea of literature as the "great tradition" of "classic works" by "men of genius." We can provide an understanding of literature as one of the places where culture has perniciously administered notions of value and desire. But literature is also one of the places where administered desire has been most purposefully contested. It is in literature that we can, immediately, expand for our students the sphere of possible pleasures and values, and allow them the opportunity to begin to go beyond themselves from the narrowness and incomprehension of their immersion in dominant culture. Such a pedagogy fulfills the real purpose of humanistic training: the growth of the capacity for critical inquiry. "Enlightenment": another glitch in the history of liberal ideology which it is pleasant to see still haunting the halls of academe. Yet another gap in the seamless text of official history through which must come those instructive deconstructive moments, authority's gaze again fallen on its own death, which must for the time being sustain writer and theorist alike.

1987

The War against Theory

We have seen in the last few years a frightening growth in the activities of ideological hacks like Allan Bloom, Lynn Cheney of the National Endowment for the Humanities, George Will, Roger Kimball, and most recently Dinesh D'Souza, author of *Illiberal Education.* This is the War against Theory to which my title refers. The much publicized PC debate is one of the fronts of this war. What I would particularly like to call your attention to is the recent drawing-up of sides in this issue. For a long time there was no coordinated opposition to right-wing attacks and slurs. There were many exemplary individual responses like that of Michael Bérubé in The *Village Voice* or the excellent analyses of the PC debate by Matthew Goodman and Elizabeth Martinez in Z, but there have been no attempts to organize opposition until recently. This drawing-up of the opposition began with special analyses on "MacNeil/Lehrer News Hour" (featuring Dinesh D'Souza and Stanley Fish), which were then continued in a feature-length debate on William F. Buckley's "Firing Line." Suddenly, the "theorists" had national spokespersons, especially the ubiquitous Fish. Most recently, many academics, assumed to be for one reason or another sympathetic to the "liberal" position, received invitations from Gerald Graff of the University of Chicago to join an organization called Teachers for a Democratic Culture. The invitation argued that "it is time for those who believe in the values of democratic education and reasoned dialogue to join together in an organization." (I have already heard Teachers for a Democratic Culture referred to as the TDC, as if it were the FMLN, or at least as if it were an inevitable participant in this contest.) Perhaps it was only because I was reading Andrei Codrescu's *Hole in the Flag* when I received the letter from Graff, but my skeptical response to the invitation was that I was being invited to join my own revolution. "Your revolution is ready, sir, right this way."

Codrescu's *The Hole in the Flag* is a personal history of a hyper-real revolution. As Codrescu describes it, the miraculous Romanian revolution of December 1989 was in fact a palace coup coordinated years in advance by the KGB, the Securitate (the Romanian secret police), and the army. In Codrescu's words, the Rumanian revolution was "a studio revolution that fooled the entire world." Contrary to the expectations of Gil Scott-Heron, the Romanian revolution was entirely televised:

> Ted Koppel found out that the dead children on the steps of the Timisoara cathedral were a fabrication. An independent videotape taken seconds later at the spot showed no bodies at all. And the extraordinary picture of the mother and her baby killed with the same bullet, seen thousands of times on all the world's TV screens, was a gross collage. A woman who had died of alcoholism had had an unrelated dead baby placed on her chest for video purposes. Someone made a bullet hole in both bodies.

In effect, the people of Romania had been summoned to or seduced by the spectacle of their own revolution. Codrescu writes: "In December of 1989 the Army and the secret police gave a revolution and the people came—to be slaughtered on live television. One of the greatest staged media events of the twentieth century happened here, using these starving people's bodies, a true theater director's dream: a play with real bodies." Of course, while one is wondering with Codrescu if "anything is what it looks like," one might suspect that Codrescu himself had been reading Jean Baudrillard during his visits to Romania. For it is Baudrillard's thesis that in the postmodern moment history/politics/revolution can appear only, if at all, as simulation. As Baudrillard writes in *Simulations:*

> Everything is metamorphosed into its inverse in order to be perpetuated in its purged form. Every form of power, every situation speaks of itself by denial, in order to attempt to

escape, by simulation of death, its real agony. Power can stage its own murder to rediscover a glimmer of existence and legitimacy. . . . In olden days the king (also the god) had to die—that was his strength. Today he does his miserable utmost to pretend to die, so as to preserve the blessing of power.

The current propagandistic "War against Theory" was launched, significantly, in "To Reclaim a Legacy," an essay written by William Bennett, the same man who launched the equally hypocritical war against drugs. This "War" is certainly of less grand proportions than the recent events in Romania. But the lessons of that simulated "revolution" are important, especially for those, like Codrescu, who would in fact like to see real revolutions in the administered realities of East Europe, or the United States, for that matter.

Are Graff and Fish running another Rumanian revolution? It was not all that long ago that Gerald Graff published a book called *Literature against Itself,* which in many ways introduced the shape of things to come in (to be sure) trashier reactionary tracts like Alvin Kernan's *The Death of Literature.* Published in 1979, *Literature against Itself* was a broadside against the politics of the sixties, against contemporary theory of the poststructural variety, and against the aesthetics of postmodern fiction. It joined John Gardner's *On Moral Fiction* as scholarly testimony against "the new," whether as theory or art. In spite of the fact that these books now seem, in hindsight, eminently fair and reasoned arguments (given the more recent scabrous mendacities of Reagan-Bush demagogues like D'Souza), they were two of the first cannon shots within the academy in the great conservative ideological struggle against the legacy of the sixties, a struggle we now think of as the era of the Moral Majority.

Stanley Fish's credentials are similarly suspect. It was only a few short years ago that he associated himself with the thinking of the New Pragmatists, a group of theory-bashers organized around the call-to-arms of Steven Knapp and Walter Benn Michaels's essay "Against Theory." Knapp and Michaels argued that "the theoretical enterprise should . . . come to an end." Fish, following "Against Theory" with his own essay, "Consequences," agreed that "theory's day is dying." He further argued that theory's merely political success within American universities is without interest because "the political is what every theorist desires to rise above." Interesting words from one who would now claim to be championing the rights of feminist, Marxist, and multicultural theorists.

To be fair, Graff, in particular, has in recent years made a sometimes riotous conversion to the camp of his former adversaries. A 1989 article about about his "conflict pedagogy" in the *Chronicle of Higher Education* quotes his explanation that he became more open-minded when "I realized I was learning more from the new theories that I was attacking than from anybody else." My merely skeptical point is that, like the apparatchik who directed the Rumanian revolution, Graff and Fish owe much of their present elite privilege as national spokespersons to earlier work that was in fact directly opposed to the thinking and interests of theorists. As a consequence, I am very skeptical about the idea that the real issues of the moment are captured by the spectacle of the opposition between the National Association of Scholars (on the Right) and the Teachers for a Democratic Culture (on the Left). The binarism that this simulated political antagonism creates has potentially dangerous consequences. In particular, I am alarmed that Gerald Graff, Fish, and the TDC have sought to soft-pedal the radicalism of recent developments in theory. Their strategy has been to accuse the likes of Dinesh D'Souza and Roger Kimball of falsification and misrepresentation. But there is an important sense in which, as the Jefferson Airplane used to sing, "What they say we are, we are." Tenured Radical? *C'est moi!* How does one get around the fact that at the heart of recent victories in the curriculum wars by feminists, multiculturalists, gay rights activists, postmodernists, and of course neo-Marxists is radical theory? If the job of the Educational State Apparatus is to provide the ideological props for a smooth integration of students into the National Factory, what Adorno called Administered Reality, the radical professoriate has refused its job description. Instead, it has prepared students to recognize and critique Western sexism, racism, homophobia, and imperialism. Because, well, in fact, those are the shoes that fit the clumsy feet of your local friendly fascist. But when a group like Graff's TDC claims the opposition while disclaiming radicalism, this leaves real left radicals with nowhere to stand. What I am saying is that this antagonism between TDC and NAS is potentially a liberal/conservative alliance against the real Left. That, my friends, is a frightening prospect.

Yet one should not make the mistake of thinking that, because the opposition between NAS and TDC is a fraud, that there are therefore no real issues at stake. As with the situation in Romania, beneath the simulated revolution is a real revolution. The interest of Bush's New World Order is in a world without leftism, a world without opposition or ideological contradiction. His effort to "Saddam-ize" American intellectuals is a response to a real situation. In fact, in the long propagandistic orgy of victory and self-congratulation that has characterized the Reagan-Bush era there has been a striking, contradictory, and oppositional politicization of the academy. Universities have remained what they were in the sixties, important bases of operations for what Noam Chomsky calls the "domestic enemy." If it is the job of the FBI to go after extra-academic groups like CISPES (Committee in Solidarity with the People of El Salvador), it has become the curious responsibility of the Secretary of Education and the director of the National Endowment of the Humanities to organize assaults on the university. To be clear, radical activity has not thrived on campus in the last two decades, but radical thinking has prospered and deepened, especially in departments of English. English departments are that poisonous lair housing that creature recently identified by George Will, the "watery Marxist."

What is at risk in the "War against Theory" is two traditions of thought rooted in the Marxist-Hegelian tradition and common to most of the political movements on campus today. The first is the tradition of critique, what Marx called "the ruthless critique of everything existing." The second is the tradition of utopic hope. Many contemporary American intellectuals reason along with Hegel, Marx, Communards, Dadaists, Situationists, hippies, punks, and cyberpunks that if there is nothing necessary or natural about the present, and change is real, then things can be otherwise. We might even allow ourselves to imagine that things can be better than they are. Certainly, poststructuralism has demolished the "naturalness" of the present social regime. And if the present can be deconstructed, this opens the way to a possible reconstruction. It is my position

3 6

that recent radicalizing tendencies in academic theory within American universities have been informed and propelled by the spirit of purposeful "play," what Herbert Marcuse called "the free play of the released potentialities of man and nature." I don't want to live on a prison planet directed by Bush's New World Order. The political crime discovered by academic Reaganauts is that much "Theory" has attempted to reclaim the world in the infinity of its possibilities. I would hope that radical academics and radical activists could stand together on this principle. Let us all say, "Death to the dictatorship of the present."

Gerald Graff replies:

What could Curtis White have had in mind when he referred to Teachers for a Democratic Culture as "disclaiming radicalism"? White could never have made that untrue claim had he bothered to find out who has joined this new organization by asking for a copy of our membership roster, now going on a thousand strong.

It is true that in the TDC statement of principles, we say that critics on the Right make "no distinction between extremists among their opposition and those who are raising legitimate questions about the relations of culture and society." In the context of the rest of the statement, it should be obvious that this is not a "disavowal" of radicalism but a criticism of the caricatures that reduce all positions on the Left to the crude slogan that "Western culture's gotta go."

It is also true that the TDC statement aims to appeal to people who do not consider themselves radicals, necessarily, but who are offended by the obnoxious misrepresentations and hypocrisies of the anti-PC warriors. For this we make no apology.

I reply:

What might I have concluded about the politics of the Teachers for a Democratic Culture by examining its membership list? Innocence by association? What I "had in mind" was the TDC's statement of principles, a reasonable place to look for an indication of the group's politics. I have lots of questions about the language there.

Graff and Jay call to our attention the fact that they don't disclaim radicalism but rather make a distinction between "extremists" and "those who are raising legitimate questions about the relations of culture and society." Well, just who are these "extremists"? Anybody I know? How cooperative it is of the TDC to acknowledge that they exist. And how does one know when one is in the presence of a "legitimate" question? As Noam Chomsky would point out, the so-called legitimate questions are usually those that fall short of questioning the fundamental right of a ruling class to rule.

There is one group that is conspicuous in its absence in the TDC's "Statement of Principles." Graff and Jay argue that "recent curricular reforms" have been "influenced by multiculturalism and feminism." No doubt, theorists of race and gender have made important contributions to curricular reform. But it is Marxist theory that has most powerfully critiqued the ideological substance of curricula and canons. Where within the TDC's description of the present moment is there an acknowledgment of the role that the Marxist tradition has played in recent curricular wars? Perhaps the most significant development in American intellectual life in the last two decades has been the rediscovery of the Frankfurt School, the reinvigoration of Gramsci in Cultural Studies, and the emergence of our original theorists in people like Terry Eagleton, Gayatri Spivak and Fredric Jameson. Whether one thinks these people and movements are Marxist, neo-Marxist, or post-Marxist, no part of their thought is possible outside of the Marxist tradition of critical thinking.

This is no secret. George Will, for Christ's sake, knows about it. So, is the TDC being coy? Is this some sort of strategy? Are we still afraid of saying the "M word" forty years after McCarthy? Or are academic Marxists "extremists"?

In the place of such an honorable (and perhaps courageous) acknowledgement on the part of the TDC, there is the spectacle of TDC charter member Stanley Fish (this is called guilt by association) flogging his Mutt and Jeff show with Dinesh D'Souza and arguing that universities ought to handle issues of race and gender as American corporations have.

One last question. How democratic is the Teachers for a Democratic Culture? Accepting $25 each from well-meaning members of the lumpenprofessoriate does not make the TDC a grassroots movement and it does not make it democratic. What plans have Graff and Jay to make the TDC a vehicle for the needs of its members, not just at the elite institutions where most of the "original signatories" reside, but at the state universities, four-year colleges and junior colleges which are most at risk of being turned into glorified vocational schools?

1992

Jameson out of Touch?

Postmodernism, or the Cultural Logic of Late Capitalism is an enormous, complex, diffuse (*garrulous* may be the right word), and influential book whose leading ideas have been richly debated among theorists since the original publication, in 1984, of the essay "Postmodernism, or, the Cultural Logic of Late Capitalism" in the *New Left Review*. Jameson's theory is that postmodernism is an expression of the essential logic of what Ernst Mandel called "late capitalism." In general, Jameson is a theorist of history as a sequence of dominant "modes of production." According to the Marxist scheme which he advocates, we are presently in the third of three capitalist moments. The first, market capitalism, describes capital in its classic phase. Its economics are local and can be experienced by a single subject; its appropriate aesthetic mode is Realism. The second stage is monopoly capitalism, what Lenin called the "stage of imperialism." Here, no one subject can experience the reality of capital because local effects have their origin elsewhere, in the colonies. The appropriate aesthetic form of this stage is Modernism, whose formal inventiveness is a corollary for the mystifying play of presence and absence in everyday Western experience. The final stage, the postindustrial or late capitalist stage, is the "purest" expression of capital. It is characterized by the absolute saturation of experience by "simulacra," by an insertion of individual subjects into a "multidimensional set of radically discontinuous realitites." Needless to say, the appropriate aesthetic of this stage is postmodernism.

The politics of the postmodern are significantly different from those of the modern because in the postmodern there is no "distance," there is no "outside" from which to describe and critique late capitalist space. All postmodern gestures are already taken up and reified as commodities. In postmodernism, we do not consume things, we consume the process of consumption itself. Postmodern artists are condemned to a futile replication of the dominant culture, or its logic. In Jameson's words, "Postmodernism is the iridescent sheen of consumerist daily life in the Indian summer of the superstate and multinational capitalism."

Finally, Jameson suggests that if there is to be any politically forceful art beyond the postmodern, it will need to be an "aesthetic of cognitive mapping" whose purpose will be to "endow the individual subject with some new heightened sense of its place in the global system." Elsewhere, however, Jameson argues that postmodernism must cure itself "homeopathically." It is no doubt symptomatic of Jameson's essential ambivalence about postmodernism that he provides two incompatible responses to its failures. The first, cognitive mapping, is plainly part of the long Marxist tradition of ideology critique and is largely modernist in its impulses (if for no other reason than that it imagines that mapping is possible). On the other hand, the idea that postmodernism might cure itself homeopathically grants postmodernism its own methods (postmodernism does not need to be cured by something outside of it). Unfortunately, Jameson is able to provide no examples of the postmodern curing itself.

I personally find Jameson's historical abstractions persuasive and powerful in their implications. I am ready to believe that postmodernism is the cultural logic and the aesthetic of something called "late capitalism" (provided that one understands, as Jameson does, that this "thing" late capitalism, is not an ineluctable essence—a tabooed "totality"—but something that specific historical conditions made possible). I am even ready to think that postmodernism is late capitalism, and is the mode of production for the "third machine age." However, I am not at all convinced by the implication that, postmodernism being hand and glove with late capital, the postmodern is then incapable of political resistance, of inscribing itself in the present moment as a "counter-discourse." What Jameson is insufficiently interested in is the idea that late capital is full of contradictions (like every other historical moment), one of which might certainly be that the logic of postmodernism can be used against the dominant order, is capable of describing both the cultural space it is in as well as alternative spaces, and is in short capable of generating its own utopic destinations. To be clear, Jameson is alert to the idea that late capitalism's development is "uneven," and that forces can exist within it which are contradictory to it. Nonetheless, the postmodern, by Jameson's account, seems capable only of a complex complicity.

For reasons that must remain obscure, Jameson is determined (and his project "overdetermined") to find that postmodern art "degrades" all its materials, reduces everything to the level of the advertising logo. Thus, there is neither critique nor the promise of liberation in postmodernism. There is only the ceaseless and saturating flow of its images (Jameson's debt to Jean Baudrillard is apparent here). In short, postmodernism is the cultural "dominant" of our time. There is a "hegemony" of postmodern discourses.

We are left with that pure and random play of signifiers that we call postmodernism, which no longer produces monumental works of the modernist type but ceaselessly reshuffles the fragments of preexistent texts, the building blocks of older cultural and social production, in some new and heightened bricolage: metabooks that cannibalize other books, metatexts that collate bits of other texts—such is the logic of postmodernism in general.

There are, however, certain aspects of postmodernism that Jameson just doesn't seem to get, or even to know about. For example, in the chapter "Utopianism after the End of Utopia" he acknowledges that there is "uneven development" in late capitalism which allows for "a kind of cultural production which is clearly postmodern and equally clearly political and oppositional." But his discussion of this phenomena—a politicized postmodern—ends lamely with this foggy description:

> it should also be noted that one finds everywhere today—
> not least among artists and writers—something like an un-
> acknowledged "party of Utopia": an underground party
> whose members are difficult to determine, whose program
> remains unannounced and perhaps even unformulated,
> whose existence is unknown to the citizenry at large and to
> the authorities, but whose members seem to recognize one

another by means of secret Masonic signals.

Here Jameson is closest to understanding the real shortcoming of his assessment of postmodern art: he's hopelessly restricted to "official" culture for his material. Unlike Greil Marcus, he has no instinct for the underground. This is especially true for fiction.

It is the sad truth that the only "postmodern" writer that Jameson discusses in any detail is E. L. Doctorow. How could anyone claim to make judgments about the politics of an art with such a pathetically small and inaccurate sample of its instances? In his defense, Jameson elsewhere argues that the "Anglo-American 'new novel'" (postmodern fiction?) was "short-lived." His logic, I take it, is that since American postmodern fiction is dead, he doesn't need to concern himself with its present, and it will be sufficient to provide descriptions of the politics and techniques of Doctorow's *Ragtime,* as a sort of relic or museum piece. Well, the discovery that they are dead can be of little consolation to those writers in the "unacknowledged party of Utopia" whose members are so deep underground that they can't be seen, no, not even by the searching eyes of Fredric Jameson.

Jameson's argument provides scholarly testimony to the history of contemporary fiction as written by New York capitalist publishers. That history goes something like this: "Between 1965 and 1973 we published postmodern fiction because hippies liked to read weird fiction. But in the mid-seventies we reexamined the sixties and concluded—through the strength of books like John Gardner's *On Moral Fiction*—that postmodernism was an 'abberation' (Reginald Gibbons). Then, thank God, Raymond Carver gave us minimalism and the New Realism. Postmodern fiction died, by commercial fiat, at that moment. Right now, we don't know where the hell we are, but we can at least say that we're making money and we're not publishing weird fiction." Thus, the world according to Random House.

But as a Marxist, Jameson has no business capitulating to this economically and ideologically tainted version of things. Jameson could very easily know, as readers of the *American Book Review* know, that the writing and publishing of postmodern fiction went on in spite of the refusal of capitalist presses to publish it. That job became the responsibility of alternative presses and magazines. Perhaps Jameson is sorry that fiction writers must live under the old fashioned hegemony of capitalist presses, bourgeois values, and Realist aesthetics. Certainly, Jameson is right to analyze what the capitalist presses produce. But what kind of Marxist is it that looks only at the dominant culture? What kind of Marxist is it that not only doesn't discuss work on the margin but refuses to acknowledge that it exists? Why isn't Jameson interested in that scene? Why doesn't he know about Sun & Moon, City Lights's new fiction series, Dalkey Archive, Burning Deck, the Fiction Collective, Fiction International, Black Ice, Factsheet Five, Semiotext(e), and *The Exquisite Corpse?* If he does know about them, why aren't they significant enough to discuss? Why isn't he interested in the way these presses contest the hegemony of capitalist presses?

Let me ask you, Fred Jameson, have you read Alan Singer's *The Charnel Imp?* Have you read Harold Jaffe's *Madonna and Other Spectacles?* Richard Powers's *Prisoner's Dilemma?* Gilbert Sorrentino's work with Dalkey Archive Press? Chandler Brossard? Gerald Vizenor's *The Heirs of Columbus?* Did you read Semiotext(e) USA and its wealth of culturally marginal pomo ranters, slackers, and pamphleteers? David Wojnarowicz? Kathy Acker? Mark Leyner? None of this counts?

It is simply inadequate and intellectually irresponsible to account for contemporary fiction with a twenty-year-old label ("fabulation") and one novel from E. L. Doctorow. If you have read the writers and publications I list above, why aren't they more important and relevant to your intellectual project than the writings of a wealthy, establishment novelist like Doctorow? Do a little homework. Take the trouble to actually know the field you are claiming to describe. Until you do this homework, you're just another Culture Cop, policing the perimeter of what will count as official culture. And stop telling people that they're dead. Dead people don't struggle. And watch your ass if you wander down into South Central Underground. The comrades in the Underground Party of Utopia are my homies. And we know your colors, Jack. True ISA blue.

1992

Cultural Studies and The Poetic

(This talk was delivered at Southern Methodist University in April of 1992.)

I would like to talk with you all this evening about the state of contemporary literature, especially fiction, from the perspective of a writer who happens also to be an editor and publisher. Of course, at this late date, twenty years into the American version of the poststructural revolution, it should be no surprise to you when I say that "literature" does not mean for me the Tradition of Great Books by men of genius providing the eternal truths of the human condition. I mean by "literature" a complex of social signifiers (like author, canon, critic, and even more suspect terms like Best-Seller) through which and for which some people (the number of whom would seem to be growing smaller) still feel like fighting. In short, the question is not what is literature at the present moment, but rather who, what organization of social forces, is presently able to define what will count as literature for our time?

It's worth noting at this point that some forces have dropped the contest altogether. Cultural studies has, at least, given everyone the impression that literature is not worth preserving because it is complicit with a particular political history and conservative (I'm avoiding the word bourgeois) ideology. It has further clearly insisted that literature's texts are no more innately deserving of study than television commercials. Literature is just one signifying practice among others and a politically debased one at that. To add insult to injury, as Mark Crispin Miller points out in his brilliant book *Boxed In,* it is the very reading techniques developed in English departments by New Critics, Frankfurt School ideology critics, and deconstructivists alike which make it possible, and interesting, to interpret, say, the "Return to Jamaica" television commercials.

Given this point of view, and I think it is in many ways a powerful and persuasive point of view, what reason is there to encourage someone foolish enough to want to write a novel or a poem? Nostalgia? Further complicity with a dead regime? I have seen no arguments, not from Stuart Hall, not from Andrew Ross, not from Gayatri Spivak, not from Mark Crispin Miller, for why literary language, what Charles Bernstein calls "the poetic," still matters. But I think that it can still matter. (I hope you still think so, otherwise I wonder why you invited me here.) My own position is that if it is true that literature has had ideological (at least conservative, perhaps oppressive) force, it nevertheless maintains the potential as a particular signifying practice for subversive force. Charles Bernstein makes a similar argument in his recent essay "What's Art Got to Do with It?" He argues first that, of course, cultural studies' understanding that the value of a work of art is determined by the same class-based dispositions that determine the differential value of styles of furniture or dress or table manners needs to be applied to itself. What privileged signifying practices enable cultural studies a perspective purer than literature's? Put another way, as Bernstein wryly does, why isn't Fredric Jameson's writing on postmodernism also a symptom of postindustrial capitalism? "The problem with the normalizing critical writing practices of the humanities is not that they are too theoretical but that they are not theoretical enough—they fail to theorize themselves or to keep pace with their own theories."

For Bernstein the poetic is "turbulent thought." "It leaves things unsettled, unresolved—leaves you knowing less than you did when you started. . . . There is a fear of the inchoate processes of turbulent thought (poetic or philosophic) that takes the form of resistance and paranoia."

If Bernstein is right, if cultural studies in its hurry to brand literature with the scarlet *I* of ideology has forgotten that the poetic as a signifying practice, if you will, is still capable of life, is still a social and signifying nexus worth struggling for, the question becomes for us, who presently has the social authority to say what "literature" is for the present?

In an essay written in the mid-seventies, "The Social Definition

4 6

of Literature," Richard Ohman diagnosed powerfully the institutional networks which determined, until that point, what could be considered "Literature." First, there was the overwhelming size and wealth of the New York capitalist presses. Second, there was the authority of a few national reviews (the *New York Times Book Review* in particular). According to Ohman, the capitalist presses and major reviews had an effective insider trading scam by which the biggest paid advertisers (demonstrably Random House) got the most and the most prominent reviews. Finally, there was the tacit intellectual affirmation of this literary version of a stock market swindle by intellectuals, especially university professors who wrote many of the reviews and assigned the standard anthologies and reading lists in their courses (these syllabi constituted the cornerstone of the official canon.)

Ironically, at just about the time Ohmann wrote this trenchant and depressing essay, the whole conspiratorial enterprise stopped working. The cultural machinery that established and stabilized literature lost this capacity. Consider this: we have not had a consensus about who the major writers of the contemporary moment are since the late sixties. As late as 1968 I think it was still possible to say that the cultural machinery for defining literature was up and functioning pretty much as it had since the late nineteenth century. We had Mailer, Bellow, Malamud, Roth, Updike, and Cheever in one camp, and Barth, Hawkes, Barthelme, Vonnegut, Gass, Coover and maybe Richard Brautigan in the other. There was general consensus that these writers constituted our contemporary canon. Now, the suspicion of the processes of canon formation are such that a critic of contemporary fiction can plausibly suggest that the best American fiction writers may be unknown to most readers, perhaps even to the critic himself.

I want to suggest that this situation, anarchic as it may seem, is not necessarily bad. But first I want to indicate how I think this situation came about. First, I think a lot of the credit (if that's the right word for it) goes to the new generation of American scholars influenced by poststructuralism, Marxism, feminism and cultural studies. Younger university intellectuals were among the first dissidents, excited by their own scathing critiques of the processes of canon formation in the various literary historical periods. The

4 7

prestige of minor or oppressed literatures rose as did the prestige of the formerly subliterary, like "Star Trek," Pee-wee Herman, and the Weather Channel. Second, for intellectuals the national book review media lost most of its credibility. The review media was found suspect in two ways: it was still interested in literature and it was politically corrupt, that is, it sought to maintain the cultural privilege of the white, male, heterosexual, upper-middle class. Hence the births of essentially oppositional book reviews like the *American Book Review,* the *Women's Review of Books,* and the *Review of Contemporary Fiction.* Finally, and most significantly, the commercial presses were successfully challenged by a whole new entity, a large, energetic, vocal and unmanageable alternative press scene. This scene, in spite of a marked lack of assets (especially for marketing, for plugging into national media channels) has survived and even thrived thanks in part to the NEA and more recently to philanthropic foundations like Mellon, Lannan and the Lila Wallace-Readers' Digest Fund. These presses are well known, but I will name a few of the more consequential: Dalkey Archive Press, Sun & Moon, Semiotext(e)'s Domestic Agents series, Fiction Collective and FC2, and the McPherson Company.

So all three legs of the triad described by Ohmann in 1975 have been challenged and weakened. The commercial presses have been challenged by the alternative presses. The mainstream reviews have been discredited by intellectuals and challenged as well by maverick reviews of the marginal like the *American Book Review.* And finally instead of keeping to their job descriptions as guardians of the great traditions, young intellectuals have devoted astonishing energies not to the maintenance of traditional canons of whatever period but to the discovery and habilitation of the so-called "minor." I think we are in a period dominated by the "minor" in the very best possible sense.

Since consensus among publishers, reviews and intellectuals is no longer possible, capitalist publishing has recently resorted to brute force. The minimalist movement and the companion "short story renaissance" in the early '80s was a massive ideological campaign to "forget" postmodern fiction of the sixties and return to the verities of American realism. Fortunately, after Raymond Carver and Tobias Wolff, there was so little real depth to this movement, this return to Real Ordinary People, that its Reich foundered within five years. Next, the most truly desperate marketing ploy in the name of literature, came the "literary brat pack," those bright-lights-big-city youngsters who drove fast, made movies and then went away, their hip pockets bulging with terrible reviews and twenty dollar bills. Their names shall not pass my lips, but their works will be piled around Michael Milliken and Ivan Boeski in that circle of hell reserved for the scoundrels of the era of Reagan gluttony.

Now New York and commercial presses are precisely nowhere, which may be as close to utopia as we will get. The hegemonic cultural machinery that has defined literature for the first seventy years of this century is paralyzed. But around its immobile figure, and out of its nowhere, comes the dancing and singing of a remarkable proliferation of voices and talents. Deleuze and Guattari speak in *A Thousand Plateaus* of the rhizome which they oppose to official capitalist striated culture. Official culture works through lines, grids, maps. Rhizomatic culture wanders like the branching networks of tubers sent off by potatoes. I think that the literary imagination has been freed by the Death of Literature to become rhizomatic. When was the last time so many distinct voices with such remarkable texts have proliferated both within the wreck of the commercial world (now that the grand old family house of Simon and Schuster is Paramount Books, the extent of that wreck is clear) and in the alternative scene? Since the mid-seventies we have had:

Gilbert Sorrentino	Kathy Acker
Bruce Sterling	Ronald Suckenick
Derek Pell	Kathryn Thompson
Rayman Federman	Eurydice
Lou Robinson	Carole Hill
Alan Singer	Jacques Servin
Steve Katz	Harold Jaffe
Michael Brownstein	Alexander Theroux
Don Delillo	Samuel Delany
David Wojnarowicz	William T. Vollmann
Fanny Howe	Jonathan Baumbach

Rosaire Appel
George Chambers
Marianne Hauser
Gerald Vizenor
Steve Dixon
David Foster Wallace
Robert Steiner
Paul Auster
Frederic Tuten
Wendy Walker
Richard Powers
Carole Maso
Steve Erickson
Mark Leyner
David Markson

Ursule Molinaro
Cris Mazza
Joseph McElroy
Kenneth Bernard
Ricardo Cortez Cruz
Walter Abish
Constance Dejong
Clarence Major
Stephen Wright
Siri Hustvedt
Stacey Levine
Don Webb
John Shirley
William Gibson
Rudy Rucker

All of this is beautifully unmanaged ideologically. How would you begin to organize these writers canonically? Which of them would you pick out as the "true geniuses of their age?" Why the hell would you want to do such a thing?

So, if we must have dead authors, dead genius, dead canon, and dead literature in order that life may live, as Adorno would have put it, then let it all die. Literature may be dead, but, for anyone who is paying attention (and the capacity of the culture to "pay attention," to notice, is the true heart of the matter), its ghostly afterlife is muscular.

1992

An Essay: Simulacrum on Avant-pop

I have recently been asked to write some short essays on cultural politics. I have stitched them together here in a shameless imitation of an essay.

I. I Attack Saint Noam at the Midwest Radical Scholars and Activists Conference, Loyola University, Chicago, 1993

In the late sixties, you will recall, one of the great impediments to successful action on the Left was the mistrust, even contempt, of the "politicos" for the "hippies," of theoretical Berkeley for psychedelic San Francisco, of, in short, revolutionary politics for cultural politics. Allen Ginsberg's famous "Gathering of the Tribes" in Golden Gate Park was the first attempt to heal this rift. Ginsberg rightly believed that the two could work together and certainly needed to work together. His optimism achieved a very short-lived realization in the anti-election activities of 1968 when the SDS and Yippie! coordinated activities, including the nomination of Pegasus the Pig for president. Unhappily, the socialist Left soon returned to its usual humorless separation from cultural politics. It ought to seem to us astonishing that a movement as marginal, fragile and small as the American socialist Left has, since the middle seventies, done nothing to accomodate or even create dialogue with punks, New Wave avant gardists, academic postmodernists, cyberpunks, political rappers, slackers, cartoon crazies on the zine scene, or independent publishers like Semiotext(e), all of which are clearly engaged in radical cultural politics.

I am going to try to provide for you my own sense of the situation on the Left, specifically the relation of the socialist Left to the academic Left and the cultural Left. I take it that the American socialist Left is a community identified with the ideas disseminated in journals like The *Left Review,* the *Socialist Review, Nation,* the *Progressive, In These Times, Z,* and the publications of the South End Press. Unfortunately, it is a discourse community that is drying up. The American socialist Left is moribund. Deathly. Its advocates, as a demographic profile, are aging veterans of anti-intervention and other New Left struggles of the past. Its politics are the opposite of infectious. They are repellant. Repellant not because Noam Chomsky or Michael Albert or Alexander Cockburn or Victor Navasky are wrong about the security state or manufactured consent or CIA intervention abroad. What is repellant about their politics is the stale odor of "state logic" about them. None of the above have advanced any description of a social organization beyond capitalism more invigorating than the oft used and dusty phrase "true participatory democracy." I find it revealing that the socialist Left is perfectly willing to continue to imagine life within the state, even the mythic United States, only more "justly" organized.

On the other hand, for radical cultural politics there is no recuperable logic of the state, especially the United States. It is precisely the state form that must die, whether capitalist or New Left socialist. As Marvin Garson, editor of the old *San Francisco Express Times* and theorist of anarchic tendencies within the Movement, wrote:

> The only way out is a revolution which is consciously determined to go BEYOND democracy . . . . The point is not to help the masses enter history but to help the masses exit from it. A mass is like a great blob of dough; it gets kneaded by one elite or another, but cannot do anything for itself. Revolution, in 1968, does not mean grabbing hold of the mass and throwing it into the left-hand pan of the scales; revolution means breaking up that sticky, shapeless mass once and for all so that no person, clique, party, or ruling class will ever again be able to pound those 200 million Americans into shape.

But the socialist Left in its relation with the academic Left has shown none of the tolerance for autonomous activity that Garson encourages. The academic Left (theorists, postmodernisits, deconstructionists, Lacanian feminists, the whole diabolical concatenation of theoretical orientations) has been roundly denounced in advance, and largely in absentia by the socialist press. Like the Left itself in establishment media, academics have not had the opportunity to represent themselves; rather, they have been represented and usually with overt hostility. The socialist Left, with Z and Michael Albert in the lead, constitute the left party of know-nothings of the '80s and '90s. As Albert put it in one diatribe against deconstruction, "If it can't be explained to a resonably intelligent person like myself during a twenty-five minute car trip to Boston, what's it worth?" When was the last time that Albert explained Marx to a hostile audience in twenty-five minutes? More than anything else, Albert and the left media can't stand the idea of intellectuals off talking to themselves in their own private language. Where, after all, is the intellectual's commitment to "the People"? But what else, Michael Albert, is a community except people who live in the same language strata? What is most striking about the new academic Left is not its usefulness to the Revolution, and certainly not its loyalty to this theoretical beggar called "true participatory democracy." What is most striking about the new academic Left is precisely its autonomy. As Dinesh D'souza has shown, the contamination of an important bourgeois institution, the American university system, by neo-Marxists, Derrideans, feminists, ACT-UP queer theorists et al. has not been missed by the Right. Professors are showing videos in literature classrooms. Someone's not keeping to his job description! Fucking scary! During the Reagan-Bush years "the liberal professor" was demonized and ranked only just behind international satans like Khaddafi, Noriega, and Hussein. (This attack from the Right against academics continues as we speak. The Illinois Board of Higher Education uses the populist appeal of putting professors "back in the classroom" as a way to curtail research—creativity?—of academics in public institutions. Its logic to "ordinary" people is simple: if you have to suffer unhappy labor, why shouldn't these professors?) And yet where academic theorists are concerned, the socialist press has few disagreements with rightist demogogues like George Will or Secretary of Education Bennet: the professors are a bunch of jargon-spouting phonies. In Will's telling phrase, they are "watery Marxists." Michael Albert wouldn't have put it any differently.

American socialism is just as notoriously impatient with the cultural politics of punk, rap, grunge, cyberpunk and other manifestations of the Youth Movement nineties style. As with the hippies, the radical politicos just don't get it. There is no interest, no sympathy, no support, and certainly no effort to communicate with ventures like *Factsheet Five* and *Maximum Rock and Roll*. Does Sonic Youth represent a politics that Victor Navasky wants to join? Well, that's why, Victor, no one under thirty-five reads your magazine.

The problem, I believe, is with the kind of logic that dominates on the socialist Left. It is the typically American, because thoroughly Puritan, logic of right and wrong. Just and injust. Western corporate liberalism is wrong and we must replace it with something right. But the logic of academic leftism is essentially the logic of separation. And the logic of punk is radically solipsistic: personal autonomy here, now, right in the middle of your hell. The socialist Left has lost touch with the logic of autonomy that once existed in the commune movement and in the theory of Herbert Marcuse. Marcuse once said:

> Now, to the organization of the New Left. No party whatsoever can I envisage today which would not within a very short time fall victim to the general and totalitarian political corruption which characterizes the political universe.

As against these forms, what seems to be shaping up is an entirely overt organization, diffused, concentrated in small groups and around local activities, small groups which are highly flexible and autonomous.

I want to add one thing here that may almost appear as heretic—no primitive unification of strategy. The Left is split! The Left has always been split! Only the Right, which has no ideas to fight for, is united.

Marcuse called this strategy "organized spontaneity."

Among the most interesting and enduring of the "spontaneous" cultural events of the eighties and nineties—and again it is one that has been wholly and shamefully ignored by the Left media—has been the explosion of independent presses. The most noteworthy of these, from a Left perspective, has been Semiotext(e) and its Autonomedia imprint. Overtly inspired by the Italian Autonomia movement of the seventies, Semiotext(e) has filled a gaping hole in the oppositional strategies of American radicalism. It has published theory (including first American publications of work by Baudrillard, Negri, Virilio, and Deleuze and Guattari), fiction and rant. Semiotext(e) USA is the most important document of the eighties for indicating the breadth and depth of American anarchic refusal of administered life. And yet I have never seen a review or encouraging mention of this press or its work in the Left press.

In short, the socialist Left press is a participant in capitalist media's effort to make the most important, and most immediate subversive activities of the moment invisible. Nonetheless, from the cultural Left, where the refusal of work goes on, one hears the mighty battle cry, "Workers of the world, relax!"

II. I am Asked if the Pen is Mightier than the Sword at the Underground Press Conference, De Paul University, Chicago, 1994

Yes, of course, the pen is mightier than the sword and vice versa. It depends on the context. Following Louis Althusser's famous distinction between ideological state apparatuses and repressive state apparatuses, it is easy enough to say that if you have the misfortune of living in Pinochet's Chile, the sword rules. In our own situation, unfortunately, the pen rules. We call it television, Hollywood and even rock'n'roll. To be sure, just beyond television's unearthly gray light is the silhouette of the cop. Baton raised.

The luxury we can not afford is to imagine that the pen is always and necessarily our ally. The pen is just another conscienceless prick, not at all unlike his cousin the sword. It is not for nothing that Kafka revealed to us, in his story "In the Penal Colony," that the pen and the sword are finally one. The machine that writes as it cuts inscribes its tale in our flesh. The name of our crime is "self-defeat."

For an "underground" press, the objective is simply "refusal."

I/we refuse willingly to conspire in our own defeat. That makes us very different in this culture. An alternative press takes up or reappropriates the means of its oppression for other purposes: autonomy, self-determination, freedom, or "fun." Or Life. Yes, the great secret of the underground's ability to reinvent itself generation after generation is that there is always a margin (sometimes a sadly small margin) of people not willing to be literally bored to death.

The quaint but effective way the peoples of our culture signal their unwillingness to be dead is captured in our pregnant expression "fuck you." Fuck you Republican and fuck you Democrat. Fuck you CBS. Fuck you Connie Chung. Fuck you Ed Meese and fuck you Andrea Dworkin. Fuck you Michael Jackson and fuck you Nirvana. Fuck you Woodstock and fuck you Generation X. Fuck you Casey Kasem and especially fuck you MTV. Fuck you Random House and fuck you Avant-Pop. Fuck you "go to school" and fuck you "get a job." Finally and most emphatically, fuck you "just say no."

So whether or not the pen is "mightier" than the sword, it remains clear that the pen (by which I mean our collective capacity for a fully human creativity, whatever that will come to mean) has a lot of work before it.

But the pen must do this work in the shadow of the PEN. We function in the shadow of DePaul University which functions in the shadow of the *Chicago Tribune* which functions in the shadow of the Illinois Correctional System. The PEN. The collective citizens of the PEN now constitute one of the larger cities in Illinois. And it is getting bigger because it is now profitable. Illinois cities now compete for the privilege of being the home to a prison. Maximum security, minimum security, we don't care. Money is all the same color green. Of course, this curious "income" is all tax dollars provided by both the prisoners and their custodians. Here, I'll give you your own money back if you'll just repress yourselves and free me of that nasty duty. It's public investment in the interest of private (technocapitalist) repression.

Of course, as Monsieur Baudrillard would point out, the most real function of the prison is to obscure the fact that the entire social system is a prison. For us, then, writers, publishers and readers of the underground, our risky strategy has to be to write ourselves out of jail. What should the particulars of that strategy be?

First, the pen in opposition must create what Deleuze and Guattari call "a line of flight." This is simply a way of thinking and acting that takes us outside the sanctioned confines of dominant culture.

Second, this line of flight or logic of refusal must have its own positive content. This is where hippy logic failed us (through its romantic naivete) and punk logic failed us (through its will to stupidity). The logic of capital, yuppie, consumption, democracy, and TV needs to be replaced with a logic of . . . well, I'll leave this space blank so that you all have something to do with your mighty pens.

III. Amerika and Olsen Ask Me to Say Something about Avant-Pop and I Use Their Invitation as an Opportunity to Continue This Meditation on the Underground

"Marginality" is not the only challenge facing "alternative" culture. It is certainly true that bourgeois culture is "louder" than underground culture, especially "vulgar" bourgeois culture (i.e., the mass media). In no way is this a fair contest. The underground press owns no "means of production" that aren't either free, dead cheap, pirated (from e-mail to sidewalks), or available through a glitch in class logic (for example, the occasional support of universities and commercial publishers—the next Larry McCaffery avant-pop anthology will come out with Viking, a far cry from squalid Black Ice Books). Beyond its obvious advantage in proportion, however, it is also true that bourgeois culture is more beautiful than so-called "alternative" culture. (This is one of those things that you are really not supposed to say. It's boho PC. It is like saying, "The problem with socialists is that they are boring.")

I am speaking of the dilemma that Roland Barthes frequently grappled with. All his life, Barthes was a fervent advocate of the politically engaged avant-garde (the Writerly), and he was the most astute critic of the bourgeois "classical" (the despised Readerly). The rude fact that Barthes bumped his nose against repeatedly was that, political convictions aside, his sense of pleasure and beauty was wrapped up in the bourgeois. The secret of his critique of Balzac, in his beautiful book *S/Z,* is that he loved Balzac. He found Balzac unbelievably sexy. And he found Balzac worthy of a book-length investigation, a compliment he never offered Robbe-Grillet. Barthes's term for this quality, this *je ne sais quoi* of the ruling class, was "the bourgeois art of life." In short, wealth and privilege have not entirely squandered their opportunities. We need to discover some of the insight of Bardamu in Céline's *Journey to the End of Night* when, destitute and AWOL from the war, he finds himself sitting in a bank lobby in New York City. And for a moment he thinks he understands the reason for wealth: so the rest of us can have something beautiful to look at.

People are not miserable or painful to look upon who:

• listen to Beethoven's late string quartets;
• read Henry James;
• visit the Whitney;
• own high-end stereo equipment;
• eat at expensive ethnic restaurants;
• own beautiful machines like Jaguar, Cuisinart and Carver amplifiers;
• live in neighborhoods that look like parks;
• own toys like hi-tech bicycles (I have a TREK 2120);
• have hobbies like collecting art, flowers, coins, cars, antiques and books;
• travel to exotic interesting places and stay as long as they like.

This is not the description of a hollow, superficial life (even though the vulgar culture of mass stupidity that the ruling class provides for the rest of us may be). Let the truth be told: the yuppies are right! Balsamic vinegar tastes great!

What one rightly resents about bourgeois culture is not its beauties but its cruelties, i.e., the things it does to make its beauties possible, i.e., impoverish and/or stupidify everyone else.

The problem for "alternative culture" in the long run is how to make itself more beautiful and intelligent than bourgeois culture. (Which will mean, I hope, keeping large parts of bourgeois culture—like jazz—which the bourgeois co-opted from resistant cultural strains to begin with.) This is where, for me, the concept of "avant-pop" makes some sense (is more than hype). Punk argues, "Look at us! We're ugly! You made us ugly! We're stupid and you made us stupid! We hate you for it! So if the world you provide us is stupid, we're going to be more stupid than stupid. If it's ugly, we're going to be uglier than ugly. We're going to stage our misery under your nose and take what consolation we can in your discomfort and the camaraderie of our performance." In the history of popular resistance to administered life, punk and its progeny were an important signal that even at its most defeated, with the Reagan-Thatcher ghouls sunk in our collective neck, refusal is possible. But the strategy of punk is, sadly, the strategy of a Caliban, the strategy of a slave.

There is no positive content to punk's politics. Kathy Acker has spoken of her efforts to write a novel *(Empire of the Senseless)* that was "positive." In her own words, "It didn't work." Acker brilliantly evokes the climate of postmodern mutilation. But who would choose to live in this mutilation? When punk sets up its home in mutilation, it is not unlike that strain of Marxism which glorifies the nobility of the "worker." But Marx's point was always to transcend work; work (i.e., selling the body as the commodity "labor power") is destructive and inhuman. Punk and the many cultural forms which have followed in its wake need to figure how to conclude their messy refusal and begin the project of reclaiming life as something worth having.

Avant-pop as a political and artistic gesture synthesizes modernist intelligence and avant-aesthetic sophistication with pop/punk/postmodern popular resistance. I want an art (hence a world) which is as smart as Adorno, as beautiful as Proust (that is, full of a passionate mastery rooted in a tradition of beautiful-making rooted in a culture of beautiful-living), and as resistant as Kathy Acker.

Examples? Like most theoretical categories, there are none to few pure examples (in spite of Larry McCaffery's avant-pop anthologies). Here's a tip which you might file under "the future": Nathaniel Mackey, *Djbot Baghostus's Run.*

As my avant-pop comrades say, It'll turn you on, Dead Man.

1995

Writing the Life Postmodern

I once imagined that I could attend a conference of the Associated Writing Programs without putting my writerly soul in jeopardy. I learned otherwise one brilliant Easter weekend in San Francisco, April of 1988. Heart's blood! Didn't I witness a horror then!

It was a conference-capping plenary session on THEORY! The panel consisted of a half-dozen well-meaning writers and poets (who shall go unnamed) and Alan Cheuse (who shall go named because he richly earned it). The sacrificial theorist was Henry Staten (author of *Wittgenstein and Derrida*). Their collective task was to make a public presentation of the facts as we knew 'em, to that point in time, about writers/poets and THEORY! How dangerous is it? What are the tolerable limits of exposure? Have spectrum analyses shed any light on artistic risk?

Among the enduring kumquats which were laid at this session, I remember as most ripe, rich, and fruitful the following:

Alan Cheuse: "What writer uses THEORY! in his fiction? No one I know of. It's irrelevant. Writers are too busy living real life, doing things like screwing each other's wives." (God knows what this leaves women writers to do. Screw their colleagues' wives, I hope.)

Emboldened by this brassy call-to-arms, the MacFlecknoes of the present, deviating no closer to sense than their august predecessor, began popping from their seats. An oily dandy with great hair like Micky Dolenz, a cravat blossoming colorfully from his entrancing poet's cleavage, and a Wildean radiance about him, said, "We can kill THEORY! We can do it! We've got the numbers! The students are in our classes! We'll organize a boycott!"

Finally, Jack Gilbert stood and announced, "THEORY! has destroyed a generation of writers and poets, and led them away from their true calling: to illuminate the human heart."

Thus the poetic soul: self-serving and macho as any literary bwana, arrogant as mice who imagine there is strength in small numbers, and poignant as candlelight cast on a shoe box in which rests a dead kitty with her favorite ball of string.

Henry Staten was admirably cool, good-natured and self-possessed during this embarrassing reveling in the will-to-ignorance parading as the Sublime. His final communication to the assembled scribblers was delivered dead-serious, almost sternly. Pay attention, he seemed to say, for just a moment, children—"Think what you like, but the writers and poets of the present who will matter in the future will come to terms with theory."

I'm telling you, it was a courageous moment. Staten was a living return of the repressed. The poetic Childe Harolds in the audience, "among but not of" the academic crowd, self-crowned with Byronic grandeur, were apoplectic with the noive of dis guy telling them that they were academics and intellectuals and therefore responsible for understanding and responding to ideas. No, man, we're angelic fluff with big balls! We're Jesus with a fifth of Jack! We're in-spired, puffed full of beeyouteeful breath!

Staten's neat trick was to demonstrate that the poetic condition in the eighties and nineties is self-loathing: I'm an academic and I hate academia; I'm an intellectual and I hate ideas.

But what did Henry "Meet Me at Delphi" Staten mean by "come to terms"? Perhaps he meant that poets need to be able to reproduce Derrida's critique of Husserl's transcendental reduction at a moment's notice on a cocktail napkin at the English department banquet. Maybe. I'd prefer to think he simply meant, "Get with it. Live in your own moment or be irrelevant."

By now everyone has received the notification:

UNTIL FURTHER NOTICE
YOU ARE IN THE
POSTMODERN CONDITION
(Address all inquiries to the appropriate French authority.)

I

I was giving one of my blustery, poetico-fictive-philosophico-polemical talks at Southern Methodist University last spring when a chap asked, "Define postmodernism and tell me why anyone should pay attention to it."

(Gayatri Spivak once provided me with a surefire method for responding to the hostile "questions" of anti-theorists. At a reception for a visiting scholar, she waited for him to sit, then circled his chair, sari rippling, farting mordantly all the while.)

Hell, I don't know what postmodernism is. Some say it's incredulity in the face of master narratives. Some the precession of the simulacra. Some the art of the intertext. Others the cultural logic of late capitalism. Most think it's MTV or the sampling of rap. Shoot, I'm too busy fighting about it to know what it is. And that's why anyone should pay attention to it: because everybody's fighting about it. It is a culturally cathected term.

In my judgment, the archetype of the postmodern gesture is Theodor Adorno's famous epigraph to *Minima Moralia,* "life does not live." Which means that a certain form of life does not live: nineteenth-century faith in the capitalist/rationalist/instrumentalist enterprise, or faith in the death of the capitalist enterprise, or faith in a mythic—high modernist—return to a time before capital. Adorno's maxim also means that life understood as a fundamental "normative" quality of being human no longer lives. In short, the Modern does not live, and that privileged modernist project called *humanité* does not live. Marx's "natural children" are all "complexed," hailed by a capitalist to-do they had no idea how to refuse. In Louis Althusser's terms, we are all "apparatchick."

Not happy theses, these, but theses.

Postmodern fiction, however, is not necessarily merely an expression of the postmodern condition. Postmodern fiction is also a strategic response to that condition. To be sure, postmodern fiction assumes a condition of "damage" (to borrow again from Adorno) and dutifully expresses that damage: we are text and getting textier. Language accelerates. If we used to chew words in the old days, a nutrient rich stuff that built strong bodies in at least twelve ways, it's all crank now, insidious binaries that we mainline, along with their insulting viruses. We've caught a computer's disease, every bit as weird as coming down with hoof and mouth.

Of course, there are some, like Jean Baudrillard, who would advise us that there is no option other than an ecstatic capitulation to the flow of signs. Thus the final destination of the human: a terminal. A terminal is an oxymoron: it is both a point on an open and flowing system (a computer terminal, for example) and "the end of the road," as John Barth put it. Terminus. It is the ceaseless and futile circulation that is the equivalent of stasis (Americans have fast cars and superhighways in order to obscure the fact that they have nowhere to go that isn't already the same place.).

Unlike Baudrillard, most postmodern fiction writers continue to carry the human capacity for resentment (although they are given no credit for this by those who worry that no one is taking flashlights into the darker cavities of the human heart). Postmodern fiction is, for its most exemplary practioners, an expression of resentment for the postmodern condition. Thus, postmodernity—like every other cultural moment—is both ideology and utopia. It is self-contradictory. Better yet, it is dialectical.

The exemplary fiction writers of our moment are not countercultural gurus convinced that we can liberate Nature from the grips of the System (hippy logic); nor are they high priests to the Imagination sitting at the right hand of a divinely appointed leader (modernist strategy—pace ol' Ez); and they are certainly not the "realist" archivists of domestic drama (the curious capitalist strategy that would seek to make fiction so banal that no one, no one at all, will want it). The exemplary fiction writer of the present moment will confront postmodern problems on postmodern grounds.

I will provide three examples.

The first is John Barth's foundational essay "The Literature of Exhaustion" in which Barth argued that the "usedupness" of the conventions of classical realism and modernism can become a means of helping the "best next thing" into being. Following this essay, Barth demonstrated in his triptych novel *Chimera* how exhaustion's empty bag, when turned inside out, begins to squirm with new life. No doubt, what the bag contains is not a Christmas puppy. It is a monster, an anti-generic nasty pasted together from animal parts which to that point had not even a nodding acquaintance. *Chimera* is a novel about pushing postmodern death-in-life (there figured as artistic and personal exhaustion/impotence) until it mutates. *Chimera* is an intimation of how one outmaneuvers a failure (call it "late capitalism") which can't be otherwise defeated.

Surprisingly, Kathy Acker's application of the cultural logic of punk (henceforth C.L.O.P.) leads to conclusions and strategies similar to Barth's. Both thematically and artistically, her strategy is to use the terms of our social defeat against the defeat itself. Hence: is our culture dead? Then I'll be deader than death. Is our culture ugly? Then I'll be uglier than ugly. Her destination, paradoxically, is new life and new beauty.

In *Empire of the Senseless* Acker creates the "pirate" as a utopic metaphor. Pirates were the first pure laissez-faire capitalists. Acker appropriates the pirate's aura in order to go beyond the piracy of everyday life under capital. Like Donna Haraway's "cyborg" and Deleuze and Guattari's "war machine," Acker's dextrous use of the C.L.O.P. allows her the risky gambit of reappropriating the terms of our collective defeat in the name of our collective renewal.

There is little *belles* about Acker's *lettres*. But she is smart in a cultural condition determined that writers stay stupid (innocent of ideas), trivial (domestic), and therefore irrelevant (no threat to the current regime).

Finally, Mark Leyner. Leyner is, as he writes in *Et Tu, Babe,* "in a certain sense, the most significant young prose writer in America." In a certain sense, "in a certain sense" he is. For, like Dave Letterman, he is said to epitomize postmodern irony, an irony without depth and wholly without commitment. However, Leyner is to Dave Letterman as Bizarro was to Superman. He is no mere homage to Dave's World. He is its anti-Christ. The *imitatio.* The false messiah.

Leyner achieved instant "cult status" with his second book *My Cousin, My Gastroenterologist,* a work whose "instant" required months of preparatory cult marketing. They flew in the cult consultants. They did power lunch with the boys from cult R&D. Kindly, at the end of it all, Mr. Leyner was relieved of the burden of being himself. He became his own toy. Leyner Я Us. Thus relieved of the obligation of the Self, thoroughly commodified, Leyner went on to use this success/his defeat against itself. Consequently, *Et Tu, Babe* is about Team Leyner, the artist as a young multinational, the first novelist to achieve offensive nuclear capacity. Commodify me? I'll commodify myself first. Leyner's comic coup is to ironize postmodern irony. By virtue of that double negative, he is impossibly sincere.

Of course, the question remains, which Leyner is it that shows up on Letterman? Leyner the commodity, or "Leyner the commodity"? Whichever the case, it is a lesson in the capacities of the Moment to see the "significant" Leyner side-by-side with Letterman. For Leyner/Bizarro has a chunk of kryptonite implanted in his pineal gland, which is hardwired to his third eye, which mystic organ saturates "the Dave" with ultimately toxic microcuries of self-regard.

II

I am going to imagine, a most improbable possibility, that I have convinced North America's writers and poets that an ineluctable part of their present condition has to do with their institutionalization within univerities. I do not at all mean by this that all writers are within universities, although a very large number obviously are. Nor do I mean that the most important writers and poets are within universities. In fact, the most interesting fiction coming through FC2 (the publishing organization I co-direct) is from people in frighteningly impoverished and socially marginal conditions. What I do mean is that, undeniably, universities constitute one of the largest environments in which we are presently allowed to work. If writers and poets are to be responsible to the World, then a large part of that World about which we are obliged to report is, for good or bad, the university. Of course, being "institutionalized" (our madness thus confined) is never simply a good or bad thing. But even in the worst case, we need to know where we are if we mean ever to be somewhere else. If the university really were an asylum for the insane, and all the poets therein believed, as many of ours do, that they were really living in another century, in a clean, well-lighted place, with a panoramic view of *le condition humaine,* then, guess what? They are going to stay in that asylum because . . . they are crazy!

So, the best question is to ask, "Where are we now?" Objectively, really, now, in the harshest light we can find. But that "where we are," I assure you, can have nothing to do with the romantic, poetic mythologies with which we too often dope ourselves. Let us ask, then, where are we? and what is the most human, most productive and—literally—the most LIVELY posture for us to adopt within where-we-are?

Well, the idiot savants of the AWP are right to think that all is not well in the academy, but that is the case for reasons they could hardly imagine. Let me provide you with a brief (and cartoonish) history of the modern English department.

Life Before Theory (or the Time of Tweed). Roughly 1930-1975. The scholar's life was predominately male and upper-class (less so from the middle-sixties on). Scholarship was a "gentleman's calling," something someone who didn't wish to dirty his hands in commerce could do without wholly upsetting class expectations. Ideologically, the dominant was New Criticism and its modernist cult of the aesthetic. Literature as religion. There was also significantly the strong residual presence of historicism/philology and its vestigial ideology of "the great books," "the classics," and "the Western tradition." As Dinesh D'Souza, Alan Bloom, and E. D. Hirsch have shown, this imperialist past is a tough little shit and never quite as dead as one would hope. Whether dominant or residual, the academy served, during the Time of Tweed, an important ideological role as the educational apparatus in which one received a proper Eurocentric indoctrination. The canon ruled supreme and unquestioned.

The Age of Theory (in which all of the above is French Fried—and to a crisp). Roughly 1975-1982. Poststructuralism and deconstruction sweep onto campus and are merged with sixties politics of various stripes, producing: Queer Theory, ACT UP, French Feminism, post-Marxism, cultural studies and the New Historicism. The most significant question for hiring and promotion becomes, for all camps, "Is he/she a theorist?" Suddenly, young faculty all avow political positions, none of which are friendly to the assumptions of the Time of Tweed and especially not friendly to the canon. This is the time of Tenured Radicals, New Barbarians, etc.

Unfortunately, the brouhaha between theorists and traditionalists, splashed across the national media, spawning repeated conservative offensives from George Will, William Bennett and Lynne Cheney, was really only a diversion from a real, and very postmodern, threat.

The Postmodern Condition (the New Regime of Performativity). Roughly 1982-present. Theory left modernity and its ideological mission not even a few shards to shore against its ruin. The postmodern moment is one of great and very rare opportunity. All is fluid. But as the molten intellectual magma cools, one particularly frightening possibility begins to take form: in the time after the end of ideology, literature has outlived its usefulness. The new word is "performance." Make your means suit our ends or else.

An instance: At Illinois State University's 1994 department banquet, Professor David Jolliffe of the University of Illinois—Chicago, presented a talk on "workplace literacy." He argued that we were in "post-Fordist" times. People on the assembly line are no longer stampers of widgets. They are stampers of widgets who need to be able to communicate about the success of their widget stamping to the next shift. "They need literacy!" Jolliffe whispered, in a near messianic tone. And producers of hi-tech windmills are no longer watched over by foremen; rather, they organize, discipline and assign tasks by themselves.

Thus, the new usefulness of the English department (by God, at last it is useful!) is purely pragmatic. We provide the margin of literacy that allows workers the power of self-surveillance. Managers are outmoded. The proletariat no longer requires a boss. For English departments have made them self-disciplining. Foucault spoke of the fascist within; this is the foreman within.

Here is the conclusion we ought to draw from this: writers and poets, let's not fight the wrong battle at the wrong time. We look stupid defending an ideologically constructed notion of literature that is long dead. Theory is not the enemy. It too is done. The real danger is that departments of English are to become service departments, functioning in the name of commerce. Across the board, those subdisciplines which have moved in during literature's waning hegemony (technical writing, cultural studies, composition/

rhetoric, linguistics/TESOL) can all easily be articulated as pure service functions to the educational factory's imperative to get people ready to go to work.

Creative writing's sad responsibility in this eventuality then would be to administer the last rites of the imagination to children damaged beyond redemption on their way to the great maw of America, Inc.

So how should writers and poets respond to this situation? I think we are really in a very fortunate and important position. As artists, people for whom literature was never only ideology but also praxis, we are in a position to be able to argue that the creation and the critical study of literature should remain at the heart of what departments of English are about, but not for the usual reasons of The Great Tradition, but because the study of the literature of the past and the production of the literature of the future requires two things fundamental to a human sociality: a critical awareness of where we are and how we've gotten to where we are, and the creation of our own future. This is what writers and poets have always done: engage the tradition within which they work, and then change it. Each new work of fiction or poetry is the presentation of a world within which we might choose to live.

III

The fault lines dividing the academic from the nonacademic, the capitalist from the anticapitalist, are not the only fractures which presently threaten the vitality of contemporary fiction. The most decisive issue concerns the rancorous split between the commercial presses and the independent presses. Since that blip on the screen which was the moment of the counterculture, when the American postmodern fiction canon—Barth et al.—was established, the New York commercial publishing houses have, by keeping faith with their accountants only, jeopardized the meaningfulness of the literary past and the very possibility for a literary future. Marx once said that one of the principal products of capitalism was stupidity. The shit that has regularly cascaded from New York in the course of the last twenty years has performed admirably its task of keeping people stupid. What pride can be taken in a line that has given us Moral Fiction, Minimalism, the Literary Brat Pack, and now Generation X? Commercial publishing has, perhaps, not been as single-minded in this task as has television, but books have offered no one solace for, let alone an alternative to, the egregious cretinism of mass culture.

I stand with the punks: BOOKS, I too dislike them.

If what is meant by *books* is the ecological disaster one discovers at the bookstore chains. Waldens indeed. Of course, there are many important writers being published by the commercial presses: Richard Powers, William T. Vollmann, Kathy Acker, Mark Leyner, David Foster Wallace, Stephen Wright, and Paul Auster. At present, the alternative presses have few writers of this stature. Of course, this "stature" is itself in large part a function of the commercial presses' access to the popular media. When the Fiction Collective published Mark Leyner, it could not get him on "Good Morning America"; Crown Publishing Company could.

Fortunately, there is much to hope from the new "underground." It is to independent publishers that young writers and readers, especially in urban areas, are turning in increasing numbers. What is finally significant in this situation is that now and for the foreseeable future, writers will have to negotiate this commercial/independent split in the process of creating their own artistic identity.

Yet another writerly dilemma was recently expressed for me by Michael Silverblatt, whose KCRW radio show "The Bookworm" is a standard-setter in Los Angeles. Silverblatt was interviewing FC2's Ron Sukenick about Ron's new book *Doggy Bag,* recently published in FC2's Black Ice book series. Silverblatt took the following intriguing position:

1) American literary culture is dead because there are no new readers capable of decoding books of literary complexity. Thus, it is not simply a question of who will read William Gaddis's new novel, but who can?

2) What is most alive and authentic in book culture now speaks

to the sexual and social experiences of a radically alienated youth (readers of Kathy Acker and Dennis Cooper). But this work has nothing to do with what we used to call literature.

3) This leaves "literary" writers and readers (including Sukenick and Silverblatt) in the untenable position of having no one to speak to except those who cannot understand them. The old literary underground is too "sophisticated" to speak to blunt post-punk receptors.

I take this to be an interesting variation on the old high culture/ low culture opposition. In this case, however, it is more an issue of the politics of intelligence against the politics of a very strategic "stupidity." If the only people interested in something other than commercial shit have adopted as their strategic refusal the C.L.O.P. (is the culture stupid? I'll be more stupid than stupid), what becomes of the old-style subversive politics of intellectual critique?

Silverblatt's position would seem to be that this fissure is unbridgeable. I tend to see the situation as opportune. First, the postliteracy of the C.L.O.P. is truly strategic and not nearly so "stupid" as it might seem. How else to explain the slacker fascination with theory? Outside of theorists and their graduate students, the biggest audience for Semiotext(e)-style radicalism (Baudrillard, Virilio, Negri, Lyotard, Foucault, Deleuze and Guattari) is among a young underground intelligentsia. (They do their book shopping at Tower Records where Semiotext(e) books are best-sellers.) In short, postpunk dissidents are not really so distant from the older culture of critique.

Second, it seems to me critically important for the older political/literary underground and the post-punk dissidents to create lines of communication. They need to speak to each other. There is something "stupid" about the intelligence of writers like Sukenick (he "doesn't get" the ideology of the Literary; he failed that course in appreciation), and there is clearly something intelligent about the stupidity of writers like Acker. What is required is a sign under which to make possible mutual (self-)recognition. Literary centers like Beyond Baroque in Los Angeles presently provide a place where those who have lost intellectual, cultural, social and sexual moorings may meet, not only as equals, but as co-conspirators. During the next cultural crisis, perhaps we'll all meet at Beyond Baroque to inaugurate the next Great Refusal. For it is written that, verily, when the universities are closed for lack of funding and universal apathy, and Henry James scholars shave their heads and have them tattooed with the sign of the Tragic Muse, then will the punks pull well-thumbed copies of Hegel and Wallace Stevens from their leather vests. They'll then go, en masse, to the nearest street-side surveillance camera and sing a capella but in a tight harmony that jars the old spiritual from *Kora in Hell:* "Literature is damned from one end to the other. I'll do what I want when I want and it will be good if the authentic spirit of change is upon it."

I am sorry if I have, in this essay, eluded my job description: discuss the future of fiction. But for me, fiction has no future that is not first socially situated. Fiction has no timeless, innocent, or removed home. The mythology of writers in their romantic bowers, alienated from the world yet obliged to report on it, inheritors of a special suffering, ennobled by a destiny fundamentally different from that of the parasite literary critic, these myths are self-defeating. Worse, they make writers and poets irrelevant. And yet, to judge from the pages of the *AWP Chronicle,* or the *Mississippi Review*'s "Workshop Issue," these myths are still very much alive.

My own diagnosis, as I have developed, would lead to these simple conclusions:

Where-we-are: institutionalized in postmodernity and threatened by the preeminent postmodern principle—pure performance. pure system.

What-to-do: BE: intelligent, critical, and creative.

I mean, by this essay, to discourage no one from their artistic projects. I mean to proscribe no one "style" over another. I do mean, assuming the garb of a Staten-like oracular seriousness, that every "Moment" has its content. We do not live in the lingering beneficence of a kindly and always "natural" sun. There is a cultural dominant, as well as a cultural vestigial and emergent. These play an often bewildering game of tag-you're-it. My point, "for the moment," for poets, writers, artists, and anyone else who aspires to something more than the status of an always elsewhere-shuffled subjectivity, is that we all must be sufficiently brave, serious, and daring to try "coming to terms" with, as Beckett put it, "How It Is."

Let us close with a little prayer for the death of the dictatorship of the present in the name of an always unspeakable future.

Amen.

1996

For four years, between 1992 and 1996, I wrote a regular review/commentary column in Andrei Codrescu's Exquisite Corpse. *Here are three of those columns which work upon ideas in the preceding essays.*

The Late Word

Why I didn't renew my subscription to Nation.

In the February 3, 1992, issue of *Nation* (our journal of record, wedged against the mendacities of the corporate media), the lead editorial praised André Schiffrin, "scourge of conventional publishing," for founding a "unique operation called The New Press, an independent, nonprofit publisher of books 'in the public interest.'" Schiffrin was the former managing director at Pantheon Books who had been fired by conglomerate meanie Random House, which owned Pantheon.

I wrote a letter to the editor of *Nation* pointing out that for the last twenty years there had been a large and lively culture of independent presses that *Nation* never reviewed, never encouraged, and rarely mentioned. I suggested that pretending that this culture didn't exist was a form of censorship.

My letter was not published.

The May 25, 1992, issue of *Nation* was devoted to books. It was the "spring books" issue. Alternative presses were invited to buy advertising space in the issue, and some—Dalkey Archive and Graywolf—did. The reviews in this issue, however, were of books published by the established commercial New York presses: HarperCollins, Simon and Shoestore, Knopf and two reviews of books from that naughty conglomerate miscreant that fired that nice

Mr. Schiffrin, Random House.

Clearly, *Nation* will take the money of alternative presses, but it won't write about them, won't review their books, and will continue to perform the function it shares with other elite institutions like the *New York Review of Books:* police official culture.

As NWA says, "Fuck the police."

My Remedy

Following an old Voodoo recipe, I plucked a rooster naked, gave him a spoonful of whiskey, then put in his beak a piece of paper on which was written nine times the word *"Nation."* I then turned the rooster loose in Saint Roch's cemetary. Within three days *Nation* was dead.

If you've recently received a subscription or renewal notice from *Nation,* ignore it. Treat it like complaints of phantom pain from someone who has lost an arm. *Nation* doesn't exist.

Censored—the News That Didn't Make the News—And Why, The 1992 Project Censored Yearbook, ed. Carl Jensen, Introduction by Hugh Downs, Shelburne Press.

One hears rumors of the New Censorship.

Living as close as we do to the Reagan eighties (when the frayed garments of the Old Censorship, the censorship of denial, were put on by the ghouls of the Meese Commission on Pornography), it's difficult to understand that the Reagan moment was awful in itself but finally phantasmagoric. It wasn't real. While we defended ourselves from Jesse Helms, our vorpal blade whistling through his shadow, something different had come up on our blind side and spilled our intestines out onto the ground as simple as opening a ziplock bag. Fortunately, we can read the future in entrails.

The horror of the New Censorship is not that something will be secret, but that everything will be known, obscene, pink and in your face. Think about it. These days, everyone's got a Mac, desktop, laser printer, e-mail and electronic bulletin board. Who wins in the nineties, Jerry Falwell or Apple Computer? In the age of the cellular telephone, you may listen to every "private" phone call in your neighborhood on a Bearcat scanner purchased at Radio Shack. The New Censorship understands that there's nothing to silence. Silence has no calculus. The Sign—what we presently call "information"—is now money's peer. Let it all flow.

Given what we know of the New Censorship, *The 1992 Project Censored Yearbook* of censored news seems quaint. It argues that "real and meaningful public involvement in societal decisions is possible only if all ideas are allowed to compete daily in the media marketplace for public awareness, acceptance and understanding." This sort of "progressive" language no longer makes me feel good. In fact, it gives me a sinking feeling. Who is this "we," the public? Is what "we" want the opportunity to "compete" in the "media marketplace"? The idea of the "public" making "societal decisions" in the media marketplace as a progressive purpose gives me the jimjams and the heebie-jeebies. I feel like I'm not being told something. What's your secret, Project Censored?

Odder yet, all of the so-called censored news in this book seemed familiar to me. Didn't we already know that the media had "sold out" during the eighties? (When had the media ever "bought in"?) Didn't we know that white-collar crime dwarfs street crime? Didn't we know about death rates among Iraqi children after the Gulf War? And Bill Clinton's involvement with Contra operations in Arkansas, was that a secret? C'mon, man, give me some juice, some dirt.

Part of the problem here is that the editors have culled their synopses from sources like *Nation, Mother Jones,* the *Progressive, In These Times,* and the *Multinational Monitor.* What reason is there to think that this book will find an audience beyond that which is already familiar with *Nation* et al.? That's okay. For my part, I am ready to be outraged twice.

Even beyond the small progressive audience that reads the above journals, in the great dark shadow of the thoughtless masses, didn't most polls during the last election indicate that people thought 1) Bush/Reagan were liars and criminals 2) the government was run by wealthy corporations 3) we're all being slowly poisoned? So what's not known? Specifics for socialist info-junkies?

7 5

Statistics for working up a righteous wrath? Restricted to an in-group of leftist savants, these secrets and conspiracies, endlessly rehearsed, become themselves pornographic. Noam Chomsky promotes a pornography of guilt. He makes a yummy fetish of betrayed trust.

The genius of the New Censorship is that it works through the obscenity of absolute openness. Iraq-gate is not a secret. The real secret is that it's not a secret. There are people who will participate in actions leading to death and worse all over the world and then tell you about it. In detail. In great detail. The truth is that everything is known, grotesquely vivid. Turn Salvadoran military death squad commanders into millionaires for killing peasants? We do that. Everybody understands and yet no one knows how to do a thing about it. What would Project Censored suggest? Put up barricades at the intersections of the media marketplace?

There is one moment of high humor in this book. In his introduction, Hugh Downs (of ABC's "20/20") argues that it was a violation of a free and open media for ABC to kill the "20/20" story on Jack and Bobby Kennedy's "extramarital affairs" with Marilyn Monroe. Downs froths, in fact, about the "libidinous behavior of the whole clan." Why isn't this an example of the "fast-food news" that the next two-hundred pages are devoted to criticizing? Go back to sleep, Hugh.

Personally, I think of Jack, Bobby, and Marilyn arm-in-arm, smiling, strolling in the open countryside like the lovers and dreamers in Buñuel's *The Discrete Charm of the Bourgeoisie*. They are committed to a very great struggle, my friends.

The Late Word Goes to the American Booksellers Association Convention, 1996

Hegel would have loved the ABA annual convention. Each booth represents a "form of consciousness," and most of the forms present this year were in open conflict with most of the others.

It wasn't difficult to see what form is currently dominant in our culture. Dell Doubleday Delacorte et al. had front and center booths with archways at their entrances like the openings to Disneyland.

But in the recesses of the hall, snarling and resentful, was everything else: New Age presses, Shamanists, computer gurus, independent literary presses, distributors of the self-proclaimed extremes (check out Last Gasp distribution in San Francisco) and of course pornographers. For two days I sought the interactive-sex video booths. I'd heard of them from a series of people who looked variously pale and spent. They said that when one crossed the boundary of the interactive-sex booth, erections ripped unbidden from the trousers of men and even (in a few instances reflective no doubt of minor technical gliches in the software of this infant industry) from the pale skirts of women. I thought I'd perch right on the periphery and play a novel game of now you see it, now you don't.

But I never did find the damn booth. One comes to understand the ABA's strategy: pleasure will be yours next time. In the place of pleasure, I found:

The Horse Whisperer, Nicholas Evans, Delacorte.
This book will be a Feature Film starring Robert Redford!
This book will be published in 19 countries around the world!

To get advance reading copies, booksellers and reviewers lined up around Delacorte's booth, feigning insouciance, but feeling, "I'm going to get me one of those fucking books that everybody else wants for reasons so obvious they are inarticulate."

When I introduced myself to the Delacorte agents (shiny young people with cleavages), I showed them my *Exquisite Corpse* credentials. They refused to give me a review copy. It was only through the most base groveling that I convinced one of the lucky few to lend me her copy for one week only.

I read it, expecting to despise its premises, its prostitution to capitalist notions of art. Imagine my surprise, then, when I discovered that this novel concerns itself with the most outrageous flights of surreal fantasy! This book is motivated only by the author's purest personal obsessions. This book concerns:
• The editor of a slick but powerful New York magazine (through her we learn not only that powerful businessmen can be women, but that powerful businessmen can have beautiful breasts).
• A young girl who loses her leg while riding a horse (through her we learn of the regenerative powers of simple faith, courage and

7 7

the love of others).

• A horse named Pilgrim (who teaches us that animals know best and that not all names in novels are symbolic; sometimes horses are called Pilgrim not because of anything having to do with the settling of North America, but because it's a cool horse name).

• And a very brave, brave, special guy, Tom, who has terrific rapport with beasts and editors of slick New York magazines with beautiful breasts. (Tom helps us to see that cowboys can be sensitive: "Your skin is so hard." "Uh huh." "Can you feel me touching it?" "Oh yes.")

This wonderful novel comes with a belt around its middle with the word "Believe" on it. I am deeply moved by this simple human appeal. And when you read this novel, as inevitably you must, and you read the sad conclusion in which Tom the Horse Whisperer dies at the hooves of a bad horse, his arms spread wide accepting his fate, you will say, "A Christ figure! At last! Where have all the Christ figures gone! Welcome back!"

For my shiny young cleavaged friends at Delacorte, I say to you, "Believe."

1992-96

The Culture of Everyday Venality: or A Life in the Book Industry

by Maggie Wehr

Here is the rap on independent/nonprofit/alternative literary presses like McPherson, Semiotext(e) Autonomedia, Feminist Press, Coffee House, Dalkey Archive, Sun & Moon, Permeable Press, Asylum Arts and many others:

- they're ineptly run by visionary but incompetent people living in former doll factories in Brooklyn or quaint Ruskinesque cottages in Oregon;
- they have no money for quality production, promotion, or royalties;
- they owe printers a lot of money;
- you can't find their books anywhere.

For those who speculate beyond the ready (and not entirely inaccurate) assumption that these publishers are simply terminal fools, the material cause of all of the above becomes quickly clear. These presses are what they are because they have no money (i.e., are "undercapitalized," i.e., are not capitalists).

Why are they "undercapitalized"? Often it's because these presses began with nothing. The only "original accumulation" these people have ever had is the impressive shelves of books which they have read and have continued reading in dead earnest since high school. So it follows that these presses are undercapitalized because these publishers are literary people and have no business skills, experience, or instincts. They don't know how to manipulate their resources so that on one bright day, lo and behold, they could have that mythic creature, a "cash reserve." But this is all well understood: nonprofit literary publishers are idealistic and poor and the only reason they're in this game is because they don't like what they see commercial presses doing to their much beloved books.

There is, however, another reason for the financial distress of nonprofit and independent literary presses, one that is less often understood even by the people running these presses. The third reason I would offer for the inadequacies listed above is that these presses are not able to function adequately because they are day in and day out screwed by the routine and hardly-worth-mentioning venality and psychopathology of everyday American business practices.

I would like to bring to your attention the composite business experiences of a single (made-up) publisher whose particulars I have pieced together from anecdotes and documents that have been supplied to me in conversations with the publishers of the above listed (and several other) real-life presses. The names have been changed even when the individuals involved were far from innocent.

The name of this composite press is the Matinée Press. It is located in Oregon, near Portland. It publishes high-quality fiction and poetry of very independent, if not particularly avant-garde, aesthetics. As its publisher likes to say, with a disarming simplicity, "I want to publish the books that I like." It was founded in 1978 by Thom Nagy, a Ph.D. in American lit who didn't much really like being a professor, who only went to graduate school in the first place because he wanted to take more workshops in writing in the local MFA mill. He went on to write a dissertation on the work of Paul Metcalf, which dissertation was promptly published by Bowling Green University Press in a quantity of 1,000 copies—772 of which were eventually sold to Daedalus on remainder and 156 of which were pulped and turned into corrugated insulators for too-hot coffee cups at Starbucks. Thom Nagy's one abiding literary conviction was that good and unusual writers should be published, good and unusual books that are out-of-print should be brought back into print, and both of the preceding should be kept in print for as long as the press could manage to survive in his roomy basement or whatever other unoccupied space he could find with an outlet friendly to his desktop publishing equipment. Not bad convictions these, as convictions go.

The first and most obvious flaw in Thom Nagy's grand plan was a) he had no money, and b) he knew nothing of the book publishing business. Actually b) was a fortunate thing because if he had known even one of the many truths he would come to learn about the book business, he would have stopped with a shudder and never begun the now highly respected Matinée Press.

But he got lucky early. He published a funny sort of postmodern detective novel called *All the Doors Were Lo(c/o)ked*—a Derridean thriller playing on the theme of the absent and the present and incidentally exposing the involvement of the LAPD in the cocaine business (that's the "c/oked" part of the title)—which, through a mostly unbelievable series of benign influences (remember when John Leonard was editor of the *New York Times Book Review?*), took off. With the modest profits from this book and the attention his astute editorial judgments were now justly receiving, Thom Nagy was able to expand the professional base of his operation. He got on decent terms with a short-run printer, found a really top-notch designer at the local art college, and—oh! *bonne chance!*—signed a contract with a national distributor. What's more, this distribution company, Froggy Native Boy Quality Book Distribution in New York City, was run by none other than the famous Ethan Walters, the man who had published so many of the great scandalous European (especially French!) writers of the fifties during the heyday of Olympia, Evergreen, Grove et al. Now Thom Nagy was working with a legend! He was working with the very publisher of his favorite books in graduate school! Didn't this conceivably mean, his large but innocent mind worked, that he too was conceivably the stuff of legend? My God, the name of Walters's company was taken from Molly Bloom's soliloquy! Talk about being in the right hands!

It is here that our plot thickens. For now young Thom Nagy and his precious love child, Matinée Press, had joined forces with the (entirely mysterious) business practices of The Book Industry.

In brief, leading up to 1996 (the point at which our thickened plot became a veritable ragout) Matinée endured the following business obscenities:

• After four modestly successful years, Froggy Native Boy fell six months behind in its payments to Matinée. Thom Nagy's creditors were screaming bloody murder. Nagy considered taking out a personal loan to cover the mess. He sought another distributor and found one. He left F.N.B. while being owed $15,000, of which he saw, in the course of the next ten years, maybe one penny on the dollar. Worse yet, Thom Nagy kept hearing strange reports of his best backlist titles turning up in bookstores in England and Europe. Had he been given a strictly accurate closing inventory report by Ethan Walters? Or had the blackguard stolen not only his money but his books as well?

• The second distributor was little better. It was Damned Right! Press of Sacramento, California, another small publisher hoping to join common force with other like-purposed publishers precisely to avoid the kind of experiences they all seemed to be having with pirates like Froggy Native Boy. Unhappily, in spite of Damned Right!'s best intentions, they were unable to succeed where Froggy Native Boy had failed because—but how could anyone have suspected this?—bookstores don't pay distributors which can't threaten them. They will pay Random House because Random House can threaten to withhold the titles from all of its many presses (without which blockbusters the shelves might appear a tad bare) but they will not pay little Damned Right! distribution because . . . who gives a darn if a few small press books aren't on the shelves? Most shocking, as Dan Paisly, Damned Right!'s guiding genius, told Thom Nagy, most bookstores claimed that they were doing them both a favor to stock their books at all and that if they were going to insist on being paid, well, the entire relationship would have to be reexamined. Business philanthropy went only so far, you know.

• Reluctantly, Thom Nagy had to look again. This time a little deeper in debt. Add another $10,000 to Froggy Native Boy's $15,000 payments in arrears. Thom Nagy made a brave move. He not only changed distributors, he hired a professional business manager, Harold S. Westman, former president of the prestigious Universal Publishers Group, someone who really knew this insidious game (for indeed Thom Nagy was beginning to suspect that this was an insidious game) from the inside. So he took a big chunk of a rare

grant and started paying out a salary (new uncharted terrain: BUSI-
NESS OVERHEAD). His most recent distributor was Smalle and
Smalle, run by Maryanne Smalle and her chiropractor husband. To
listen to Westman, it seemed like a good deal. She had lots of sales
reps, good relations with the chains, and what was clearly a very
determined disposition. Only a few things made Thom Nagy nervous. The catalogue had things in it like the *Bridal Gown Creative
Bridal Guide Annual.* And Hand Jive, publishers of not-so-vaguely
seamy cartoon books. And Great Day in the Morning Press which
appeared, if Thom Nagy understood, to be devoted to books about
breakfast cereals. But he was assured by his heady and confident
new business manager that Maryanne Smalle was a very shrewd,
hard-nosed and capable business woman and he was in good hands.

Okeydoke, said poor Thom.

Well, in the course of a very usual four-year period of moderate
success, even the "hard-nosed" Smalle fell behind, one month at a
time, and Thom Nagy began once again to suspect that he was going
to get screwed. To make matters worse, Harold S. Westman took a
sudden powder, claiming that the years of publishing stress had
taken a toll on him and he was heading out for his cabin (for he had
a cabin) in Idaho. With more than a little trepidation, Thom Nagy
began looking into the funny notebooks in which Westman always
seemed to have his nose. The notebooks with the lines running
north to south, some of them red lines, and all the blizzard of numbers. What could they be about?

It took awhile but it didn't really take a long while, because
Thom Nagy was finally a bright guy. He concluded that, quite on his
own, Westman had dug yet another tidy $20,000 hole for Matinée
Press. The infrequent checks from Smalle and Smalle had gone not
to pay printers (whom Thom Nagy could practically hear breathing
very hard right outside his not-very-substantial door) but to pay the
part-time salary of Westman's little crew of mostly unneeded assis-
tants (one of whom was apparently a semi-alcoholic, near-street
derelict who spared Thom Nagy the unpleasantness of firing him by
abandoning his car at a local intersection and running off, literally,
for the hills from which he was finally dragged all disheveled by
police, counselors, and family). This same semi-alcoholic young
man had also misplaced several checks from Smalle. Westman had

of course continued to receive his own salary until the last untidy dollar was gone. Finally, Thom Nagy discovered in the back of one of the notebooks in Westman's pencilled scrawl a list of curious IOUs to authors from whom Westman had essentially misappropriated monies intended for royalty and foreign-rights payments. Between the money paid to semi-alcoholic and otherwise useless employees and the money filched from authors to float the nonetheless sinking ship of Westman, Thom Nagy found himself another (should he say self-inflicted?) $20,000 in debt.

Who in the world, he wondered, would be dumb enough to print another of his books?

Fortunately, at about this time Distinguished University Press, long an admirer of Nagy's skillful and caring editorial vision, came along and offered to help. They could take over not only distribution but also marketing and promotion. They were nice people. Nothing like the aggressive and punishing Maryanne Smalle. Thom took out a big loan (part of which was secured by his little red Honda Civic) to float the press during the transition, held his nose, said his prayers, and jumped.

It was at this point that Thom Nagy met another player in this tale of the psychopathology of everyday American business practice. It was called "a distributor's contract." He had signed one, he dimly remembered, way back when with the bearlike figure of Harold Westman looming over him, chuckling, lighting one of his ubiquitous pipes, and bearing the brave mien of a man who knew what he was about. But what was in the contract, well, Thom Nagy couldn't say for sure. But Maryanne Smalle could. Apparently, even though she was six months in arrears in her own payments to Matinée, she was still well within her rights in creating a reserve against returns from bookstores up to 25% of the previous year's sales (never mind that that was 25% of money over half of which she had never paid to Matinée to begin with). Thom Nagy was what we used to call flummoxed. Still, things began to clarify for him. Big things. Things about the nature of an entire so-called "industry." He realized for the first time the gigantic stupidity of basing an entire multibillion dollar industry on what was essentially "consignment" terms. Local honey producers might leave their locally made honey at the supermarket on consignment, but an entire na-

8 4

tional industry? He realized the farcical, laughable dopiness of imagining that the comical crew of incompetents—what Distinguished University Press flung to the far corners of the continent and referred to as "Sales Reps"—actually knew anything about any book that ventured beyond indiscretions concerning Dennis Rodman's disinclination for cunnilingus. Thom Nagy could train his pet cockatiel to do a better job.

Closer to home, Thom Nagy wondered how it was possible that he could be said to owe Smalle and Smalle 25% of total monies most of which Smalle still owed him. It seemed metaphysical to him. Sort of like what he remembered of Kantian antinomies. But Smalle seemed to know exactly which came first, the chicken or the egg; what came first were Thom Nagy's eggs, all (or both) of them. Ms. Smalle was always capable of reasoning through Thom Nagy's objections, in her brusque and efficient way: "That is what the contract allows and that is what I am going to do."

"But don't worry," she cajoled, "you'll get it all back in one year providing that there are not large returns."

In short, Smalle and Smalle kept the previous six months sales as a debt to Matinée and then proceeded legitimately (which is to say, contractually) to keep the next three months of sales as a reserve against returns. Only one other thing you should note here: nothing in the brilliant contract devised by Harold Westman required Smalle and Smalle to keep this so-called reserve anywhere other than in its own quite active in-and-out checking account. For, indeed, poor Thom Nagy wouldn't know an escrow account from a rock dove.

For a while it appeared that Distinguished University Press would succeed so wildly where Smalle and Smalle had failed that new revenues would keep him afloat and important into the next century. But then, and this brings us up to the present, on one sad day in the summer of 1996 he received his sales report from Distinguished U. There was bad news. Returns had been heavy. Thom Nagy sighed. Well, it was nobody's fault. We got the books in stores and they just didn't sell through. He looked at the lengthy returns pages. And it began to dawn on him. Page after page with the unmistakeable imprimatur of the enormous bookselling marvel, coast-to-coast, a thousand stores, the Behemoth and Nimrod Co.

Then he looked at the ISBN numbers for the books returned. What were these numbers? He didn't recognize them. Were they even his books? He looked through his catalogues. At last he found them. Books sold in 1993! Books sold in 1992! Books sold in 1982! It was as if Behemoth and Nimrod were in fact simply an enormous and very constipated digestive system that had with an imponderable energy one day found its autonomic system and with a wild convulsion that began on the west and east coasts simultaneously rolled thousands and thousands of books that Thom Nagy had imagined sold for years back to the publisher. There was one book returned by the hundreds that Smalle and Smalle had only sold five hundred of in the first place. Thom Nagy had to wonder: had anyone ever actually bought even just one copy?

Nagy was unhappy. He put his sad little publisher's head in his sad little editor's hands. Then, like you see in movies, like Jimmy Stewart realizing something really bad, it came to him. These thousands of returns had gone to the wrong distributor! They should have gone to Smalle and Smalle, who—after all, dear God!—had the theoretical reserve. Now he was going to have to pay once to print the book, twice to protect against the book's return and thrice to accept the return itself.

Believe me, Thom Nagy's phone started getting a workout. He called Smalle. Would she accept the returns? No way. Too complicated. Would only cause more headaches. Would she then at least pay him what she owed the press? Sorry, we don't have a dime. Smalle and Smalle had just received its own returns from Behemoth and Nimrod one hundred times the size of Matinée's little sum. Distinguished University Press, could you please ask B&N to consider redirecting its accounting to Smalle and Smalle? Sorry, not worth the effort. B&N is probably not really aware that it even carries your titles. Best not to call too much attention to the fact. It could affect future sales.

Oh but there were other fantasies. The independent bookstores of America would rally to his cause. Why, he'd be the first publisher to refuse to sell to Behemoth and Nimrod. He'd sue Smalle and Smalle. Reviewers would support him. They'd help him tell the truth! And he'd place an article in *Nation* exposing the whole sad mess. In fact, he immediately picked up his last issue of *Nation* and, lo and behold!, it was devoted to the corporatization of America. Damn it, he had allies after all! But then he turned to the back of the issue.

And there it was.

The future. A sadder but wiser future, to be sure. For the entire back page of the anti-corporate issue of *Nation* was an enormous paid ad (oh paid it was with money Thom Nagy was sure had filtered to the bookselling giant from some of his own *stolen* money (yes, *stolen* was the word he used now; he was getting a little paranoid (not to mention pathologically obsessed!))) bought by "America's Bookstore," Behemoth and Nimrod.

Which, he wondered, would be more important to *Nation:* his little virtuous tirade or Behemoth and Nimrod's $$ for full-page ads?

His little house of cards crumbled. Who was he kidding? *Nation* wasn't going to print his exposé. And if he wasn't going to do business with Behemoth and Nimrod, he might as well get out of publishing altogether. The chains were over 50% of his sales. And the independents? He checked it out. Only one of the so-called major independents in the whole of these United States had ordered more than two copies of any book in his spring list. The independent bookstores were out to save one thing: their own asses.

But wait a minute. One last hope. Reviewers. The people who had written about and loved his books, supported his quixotic endeavors for years, they'd rally to his cause. The *Village Voice* could organize a benefit! But once again, reality checked in. In fact, the great independent *Voice* hadn't run a full review of one of his books since the earliest days of the press (days which could only now seem to him wickedly blessed). And, to make matters much worse, he was having a peculiar kind of trouble with reviewers of late. It seemed that many literary reviewers also fancied that they were writers. No less than five important reviewers had submitted books to Thom in the last two years. They had all been rejected. This had put a not-so-curious damper on their collective enthusiasms. In fact, Thom suspected that he'd been blacklisted at some places. For example, *Hava! Java!,* a new glossy big-city weekly, had stopped running reviews of Matinée's books when in the past he'd practically been able to wallpaper his office with the glad tidings. The culprit here, L. A. Salieri, had actually written to Thom about it:

Dear Thom:

Even though I think doing an interview with you for *Hava! Java!* is a great idea (it's terrible the things that have happened to you in the book business!), I am temporarily declining the possibility. For the reason that Matinée has not made any decision on publishing my manuscript. I will be changing my mind on doing the interview if the above situation is dealt with.

In fact, Thom had written a very (very!) generous note of rejection to the semiliterate Salieri. Guess he wanted Thom to try again. Even now, though, the sentence fragments and other instances of creeping idiocy made Thom a little ill. This was the kind of person that Thom counted on to carry his cause to the public: a perfectly self-deluded and probably crazy dolt.

From which many awesomely accumulated truths, Thom Nagy could conclude but one thing which became the one great, grand inevitable Truth of his career in the Book Industry: the only entity that really has to live by its contracts, the only entity that is really expected to pay its debts, and the only entity that will certainly have to pay interest on its outstanding debts is absolutely the smallest entity in the system. Namely: precious Matinée Press.

The wild expansiveness of this insight literally floored Thom Nagy. He pitched backwards and might have received a nasty blow to the head were it not for the fact that he fell right on top of a pile of submissions, hundreds of them, sent in just the last two weeks and not yet removed from their spongy mailers. On this cushion, the extraordinary naivete of the world's writers, he could always depend.

Maggie Wehr is a consultant with a long history working with arts foundations and independent publishers in the Pacific Northwest. She is devoted to helping nonprofit presses develop long-range plans. Matinée Press has just hired her.

1997

I Am Artist; I Make Beautiful Things:
A Credo of Sorts Concerning the New Beauty

"In his work a purely musical residue stubbornly persists."
Theodor Adorno on the music of Gustav Mahler

I'm embarrassed by my title. It has gotten difficult for me to say the words *art* and *beauty*. These two words—when I forget "what I'm about," as the British say, and use them—make me feel antique, precious, unhip, and not a little stupid. What will my theoretician friends in the English department think? "This poor nudnik. Where's he been for the last twenty years?" My embarrassment feels like an apology. I can feel an apology rising up from out of a wounded organ that stretches from my intestines to a hinter region of my brain. I think my spinal cord wants to make amends. Here it comes: "I know that 'art' and 'beauty' have been deconstructed, demolished and otherwise banished from any thinking persons lexicon," I begin. I'm looking around now, hoping to see those reassuring nods that say, "Maybe he won't have to sleep all the way on the other side of the compound fence. With the wild animals. With the dogs we don't like." I get one or two such nods. I continue: "But I don't mean by 'artist' and 'beauty' what you think I mean." Sure buddy. Whatchoo say.

Now I make the truly desperate dodge (the substance abuser at the apex of a family intervention): "I don't want to be an Essentialist any more than you do."

Well, now I've said it. "He doesn't want to be an essentialist, Harriet."

In general, I am in agreement with the drift of ideas in the

United States (i.e., the drift of Theory) in the last twenty years. What a little astonishes me, however, is that although the work of artists has continued unimpeded during this time, no new or more appropriate vocabulary has emerged in the place of our admittedly Romantic understanding of Art and Beauty to describe what it is that artists do. Artists have continued to do what they do, but they have done what they do in a sort of embarrassed silence. Artists have not known how to talk about what they do without either seeming to denounce themselves (never a comfortable position), or denouncing the conclusions of the last twenty years (in essence returning with a noisy curmudgeonliness to the high Aestheticism of Modernism, American Realism and the New Criticism). In short, there is no postmodern aesthetic. The postmodern knows not how to talk about its beauties. To be sure, there are accounts of postmodernism as a plundering anti-aesthetic of the pastiche, but there is no positive account of a postmodern artistic "ought." Unlike any previous generation of artists, no artist who is actually a member to the Moment can say to either peer or apprentice, "This is how it ought to be done. This makes it beautiful."

But, as we know, artists are usually awkward when it comes to explaining why it is that what they do is important. Fright and urgency have been added to this awkwardness by the noisiness with which politicians, especially of the Newt/Jesse Republican Right, have asked, "Why do we need these guys?" Doubly frightening (do you hear that little thin voice?), theorists have begun asking, "Aren't these artists and so-called creative writers just a front organization for capitalist ideology? Aren't they the last faithless refuge for Bourgeois Humanism?"

So here stand the artists feeling, paradoxically, like new kids on the block they've lived on all their lives. To their right conservatives tell them they are immoral and should not exist except as a kind of ongoing anti-Americanism (unless, of course, they are willing to paint what has already been painted, especially if they paint what Norman Rockwell already painted, or—as Newt Gingrich has requested—if they write like Mark Twain (fat lot Newt knows about Twain's heretical misanthropies)). In front of them, liberals reassure them of their value, but in language that reminds them of Hallmark greeting cards—"You make visible the eternal human spirit!"—which language makes them sick of life and eager to swallow their paint solvents. To their left are socialists and leftist intellectuals who complain peevishly and narrowly that their work is politically offensive to just about everybody. The artists try to speak, to respond, but their voices sound now like the high whine of a vacuum cleaner with a dust bunny clogging the hose, or a food processor working on unshelled walnuts. They are unintelligible, especially to themselves.

But, as I've said, there's nothing new in being an artist and being uncomfortable explaining what it is you are and do. The reason for the discomfort simply changes from period to period. Let's look at the logic behind the "artist question" (and the implied final solutions) for our own period as it applies to the conclusions of those who ought to understand art best, art's critics. The present discomfort of artists over their status as Artists and their embarrassed relation to something called Beauty are the result of at least two trends in critical thought which have, I believe, been applied to the activities of art in an extreme and very unhappy way. Criticism has fallen over backwards to avoid falling on its collective face. As Ezra Pound wrote (and who quotes Old Ez, *il miglior fabbro,* these days?), "It's easy to go to extremes, hard to stand firm in the middle."

Anti-essentialism. The exuberance with which younger American critics have embraced the philosophy of "anti-essentialism" (if there is a philosophy that one could call essentially anti-essential) has been at times chilling. Anti-essentialism was the conclusion of a complicated logic found by American critics primarily in the work of Jacques Derrida. Derrida argued (and argues) against "the metaphysics of presence," and "transcendental signifieds," and "the purveyors of Truth." Thus it has seemed easy to conclude that notions like "Beauty" or the "Artist" appeal to a Romantic, ideologically bourgeois and always and everywhere complicit (and therefore culpable) philosophies of the Real. Critics working under any one of a number of deconstruction's many mantles (especially New Historicism and Cultural Studies) have demystified and debunked (depending on whether it was a Romantic or ideological claim being made) the idea that the notion of Beauty has a transcendental or otherwise constant and enduring Being.

The consequence of this logic for those in the field (as anthropologists say) is that few of us have escaped the frightening (for the traditionalist), powerful (for the theorist), or anxious (for the artist) experience of being informed that concept X (Truth, fact, Reality, sense, knowledge, power, our dear friend Beauty, but you can fill in the blank) was an example of "essentializing" and therefore an already defeated concept, defeated before the discussion had even properly begun. This has had, however, the unfortunate consequence, to paraphrase Fredric Jameson, of dismissing from the field exactly the ideas about which one had come to argue. For example, in Marxist philosophy simple anti-essentialism has created a most intense and paralyzing incongruity. Because Marxism's historic appeals to notions like "freedom" or "exploitation" or "alienation" or "humanity" have been so thoroughly castigated as "essentialist," Marxists like Althusser and post-Althusserians like LaClau and Mouffe have found themselves in the (from my perspective) untenable position of arguing resistance to capitalism or the late-capitalist state for reasons that they cannot themselves articulate, have in fact rigorously forbidden themselves from articulating or appealing to. This has led to an ethical impoverishment of the Marxist tradition whose beggarly apotheosis is the glib and fatal thought of Jean Baudrillard.

Artists and critics presently find themselves in much the same untenable position. They can't simply assert the reality of Beauty as some sort of unearthly absolute (the Sublime) and no one seems to be able to articulate an alternative (although they exist), so artists and critics maintain the position of an officially embarrassed silence. An "Idealist Embarrassment," as Hans Robert Jauss once claimed of Marx's work.

As with the Marxist dilemma I have described, artists are left without a vocabulary to describe why they do what they do. Why make art? What is the role of art/beauty beyond endlessly self-deluded puppet of ideology or, on the other hand, politically correct proponent of obvious virtues? They are also left without a way of judging how one piece of art is better than another. Without a way of talking about what it means to be an immature, maturing and mature artist (maker of a particular kind of something). Any working artist must consider both of these things as a daily and ongoing function of his/her work. I'm doing it this way rather than that because it is "better" this way. What do you mean by "better"? Never mind.

The second theoretical tendency within recent North American critical thought that has tended to make the discussion of art and beauty nigh impossible is the emergence and subsequent dominance of the socio-political. So art about AIDS or racism or corporate hegemony or patriarchy has a de facto relevance, importance and justification quite apart from whether or not there is any artistic "value" (let's call it) involved. For instance, a recent public relations project by the Guerrilla Girls argued that "when racism & sexism are no longer fashionable, what will your art collection be worth? . . . For the 17.7 million you just spent on a single Jasper Johns painting, you could have bought at least one work by all these women and artists of color." There follows a list of about fifty artists.

I would hasten to agree with the Guerrilla Girls that the art market is the absurd toy of the ultra-rich, although I find it curious that the G. Girls seem to have no quibble with the ultra-rich as such, just with the politics behind how they spend their money. I'm not sure, however, that that market is absurd because it is sexist and racist (or more so than any other institution you might name). Worse yet, the logic of the G. Girls creates a complete superimposition of the political on the aesthetic. The Guerrilla Girl's appeal in the name of artists finds the aesthetic irrelevant.

One of the best articulations of this situation is Julie Caniglia's "57 Cultures and Nothing On" which appeared in the *Minneapolis City Pages* (April 24, 1996). Caniglia argues that art has become "a refuge for the creatively challenged."

> In the art world as elsewhere, the multiculturalism that appeared so revolutionary 10 years ago has curdled into a fractious politics of identity, resulting in a new and, for the most part, incredibly banal didacticism: work that "explores" this personal issue or "documents" that social problem, that "provokes" the viewer regarding the artist's identity, or "confronts" the artist's traumas (usually of childhood origins).

As a consequence, she concludes, "As art gets parsed into a multitude of niches based on identity, it follows that the standards for judging such work are lowered, eliminated, or qualified into irrelevance."

It is in this way that a finally trivial artist like Judy Chicago can become "important" because she engages feminist themes. Does feel-good equal good? Does the fact of AIDS make a tedious melodrama like *Longtime Companion* important cinema? Is the solemn *Safe* by Todd Haynes "good" because he's correct: there are toxic pollutants in our environment? Amy Tan is a serious novelist . . . why? Of course, art about right-wing politics (like skinhead rock) is not art at all. That's a hate crime.

I'm perfectly happy with the conclusions of these artists (or "cultural workers," as some would prefer to be called) as political conclusions, but appalled that they are what pass for aesthetic judgment. I don't think that we on the Left have even begun to acknowledge how impoverished our thinking about art is. If the kindest thing we can think to say about art is that it has a socio-political function (when it is Correct), then we are simply and merely advocating art as an assertion of political will. We are asking for that most despised quality, "program art." Moreover, we lose in this way art's artiness (a conclusion that the work of anti-essentialism made possible and tolerable and hardly worth mentioning). We lose the history and the tradition of art's "making" and, significantly, art's "doing" (that is, art's capacity for having its effect not through didacticism but through a formal as well as political rhetorical engagement with its audience). And whether we acknowledge it or not, we are saying that art is irrelevant. Well, if that's the case, let's just all go on down to the demonstration and get our fair share of abuse that way.

We also need to acknowledge the often painful fact that politically oriented critics have often and frequently and vociferously argued against the "content" of much contemporary art. The censorial thrust of much of these arguments is obvious to artists if not to critics. For example, in 1994 at Illinois State University, the University Gallery curator, Barry Blinderman, brought in an exhibition of paintings by Mike Cockrill. The paintings depicted adolescent and pre-adolescent girls in a variety of precociously sexual poses. Of course, the scandal that erupted focused on the suggestion that these were paintings which existed purely for pornographic purposes. You got naked little girls, you got pornography. None of the exhibition's critics and, most unhappily, none of the exhibition's defenders seemed interested in or able to "read" the paintings. No one seemed able to recall that a whole lot of art works not through sincerity (the artist's "statement," his/her "witnessing"), but through irony and metaphor: saying one thing and meaning another. Our preoccupation with "locating" everyone's "position" in a wholly political grid has had the tendency of making criticism formally illiterate, and, worse than that, dead to art's pleasures. Everyone in the local community was talking about Cockrill's paintings, but no one was looking at them with much care. We had been humiliated by a political critique into a shamed averting of our eyes from exactly that which was meant to be the focus of our attention. "Will you 'gaze' upon the paintings?" became a kind of political litmus test that precluded (not to mention occluded) all other discussion. In fact, by my—very nervous, I admit—reading, the show was exactly about libido and complicity. "What gives us pleasure is corrupt." Roland Barthes, whose *S/Z* is a great textbook of guilty pleasures both sexual and literary, would have understood these paintings. But then he was neither a simple anti-essentialist nor politically correct.

What made the local "progressive" community intensely nervous was not simply that Cockrill was depicting adolescent sexuality. That is done routinely and without scandal in television, advertising, and mass-cult cinema. Those depictions are "acceptable," in a pragmatic sense, because popular culture is its appropriate place. We expect the "market" to be evil. What made Cockrill's critics nervous was that his paintings were being presented within the institutional space of a university and a museum. The simple fact of their presence within that insititutional space implied praise for the work and, implicitly, praise for what was depicted. But, of course, universities, museums, and their related institutions (funding agencies, etc.) are precisely the places in which the socio-political has chosen to exhibit its own virtues. It is these institutions which confer upon feminism, multiculturalism, and gay/lesbian activism the mantle of its "goodness." What Cockrill presented was not PC's "sincerity," but a highly charged, ambiguous, and, nota bene, seductive visual pleasure. I can't help but wonder if it wasn't precisely the success of the paintings, their visual "excitement," that accounted for the intensity of the criticism directed at them. When asked what a more appropriate vision of adolescent sexuality might look like, one critic replied, "A picture of a girl sitting with her mother," a comment which I took to mean, very much against its will, that "Satan gets all the good lines."

Whether from the Left or the Right, there is nothing obscure or ambiguous about our political convictions. From whatever direction, our political convictions are vulgar (caught in a primitive rhetoric without a complexity adequate to the complexity of the world it would seek to diagnose). One joins forces with politics in the way that one joins forces with a wave: it's going to take you where it's going to take you, there is little or no chance of amending it, and it will likely toss you out uncomfortable and unhappy ("fooled again," as the Who said) when it has run its course. It is precisely art's obscurity, its unwillingness to capitulate to simple formulations of "position," that makes it suspicious to Politics. What are artists doing? What art is "doing" is creating the possibility for meanings that cannot be limited by the simple sense of the world provided by politics. What feminism, multiculturalism, the Christian Right, Democratic liberals, and anyone else with nothing more than a "position" are saying to artists is: echo our ideas or else.

Against the abstractions of the conservative/Romantic ideology of art as essential and timeless reality (delivering the goods on eternal human verities) and against the self-defeat of knee-jerk "anti-essentialism," I would argue two things, the first of which seems to be bright in its simplicity and the second more subtle and shaded. The two are intimately related.

Point the first: Art as such is nothing more than its own very human traditions. That tradition is implicitly dialectical. It is complicit in nearly exactly the same proportion that it is subversive (which is why history, including art history, is really long). It seems to have a motor that keeps it always changing, but never changing so much or so quickly that it moves from "fish to fowl" in one moment. It is in many ways the tradition of our humanness itself (art articulates what it means for humans to be human). This is part of why our best artists have the most highly developed moral imaginations and the greatest "negative capability" (the power to imagine what it is like to be other people, maybe even especially other bad people). Art should not be presumed virtuous, nor should its role be presumed to be instruction in virtue. Art is not the province, as Dave Hickey writes in his brilliant little book *Invisible Dragons,* "of right-thinking creatures who presume to have cleansed its instrumentality with the heat of their own righteous anger and to be using its authority (as the Incredible Hulk used to say) as a 'force of good.' " Rather, art is about the morally unsettled relation of the work to its audience. The work uses its "beauties" to seduce the viewer to literally "incorporate" with the work, to take on the work's "body," to feel its pleasures. This is, needless to say, an often frightening and usually dubious process, but it is also the secret that Shakespeare's *Richard the Third* and even, God help us, Bret Easton Ellis's *American Psycho* know that the forces of artistic/political propriety don't.

To cut ourselves off from art and its "beauties" by arguing that they are "essentialist" or politically evil is to cut ourselves off from ourselves. The human project is the ongoing discussion of what it ought to mean to be human, and art is the most benevolent site for this discussion (much kinder than the floor of the House of Representatives and certainly kinder than the anteroom to the House where corporate lobbyists draft the legislation that will legally orient ourselves toward ourselves and our world until the next crippled term of the next crippled Congress begins).

Thus, art provides a tradition of the human from which we should not want to distance ourselves. It is in fact exactly the "rag and bone shop" that we ought to sink ourselves into. But we cannot immerse ourselves in that tradition without being first able and willing to read it and to engage it formally. We cannot read it without a close familiarity with the history/tradition of which it is a part. This immersion in history gives art a complexity that irritates the impatient reader/observer who is merely convinced of his/her own ideological "position." What, for example, makes Mike Cockrill's paintings interesting art is that they mix equal parts of horror and indulgence. The paintings neither bluntly blame (as child abuse advocates might like) nor entirely volupt (as pornographers might like). The paintings create emotional, libidinal and political insta-bilities. The same sort of engagement/distancing with the technical conventions of representation (commercial, pornographic and beaux arts) can be discovered in the formal strategies of the paint-ings.

In short, to abandon art's artfulness is to abandon human his-tory, the tradition of the human as an ongoing and internally con-flicted (dialectical) project, in the name of a cloistered desire for immediate "totality" (the world this way once and for all). Thus, we should speak of art as the most central place where we have carried on an enduring discussion of what we are and what we want to be-come. Good art demonstrates respect for the human world because of the painful/beautiful history that has brought us to this point, and also shows a certain contempt for that world because the image of a more "desirable" world can always be suggested. An awareness of and engagement with the formal history of a specific genre is an essential and inevitable requirement for this process.

Beauty.

First, poststructuralist thought is quite right about it. "Beauty" has no independent, enduring, unique, timeless being. It has no "presence" separate from (that is, transcending) immediate histori-cal human contexts. So we shouldn't be interested in what it is but in what we say (and have said) it is. (See Morris Weitz's still-rel-evant essay, "The Role of Theory in Aesthetics.") This corresponds roughly to what Foucault called historical "fact": the "it is said." History is not composed of facts; it is composed of what people say (especially in legal, medical, and otherwise "official" documents). In much the same way, Beauty is not a fixed quality; it is an ongoing dialogue.

Any given piece of art is always a composition of history (what has been said) and the moment (what the artist would contribute to what has been said even if that only means basically repeating what has been said (i.e., the boring)). Art has both an ideological and a utopic purpose and every "beautiful" piece of art will find a way of rendering both. This is, in part, what Derrida's concept of "closure" must mean for us. Whatever we do, we will work within the history of an ongoing (and often failing) project called "the human." This is, in Hegelian terms, a Spiritual exercise.

Something is beautiful when the artist works collaboratively with an inherited past, ingeniously reveals again that history within the work, but then—ah! the bright wings!—opens, allows that familiar world to unfold unfamiliarly (Shklovsky) as either a) the known world re-understood as desirable after all (the ideological) or b) a new world, surviving on bits and pieces of the past (all its parts are borrowed), and erupting as an alternative world we might inhabit (the utopic).

What's an example of a.? How about Gerard Manley Hopkins? He worked within the dying tradition of the rhymed and metered lyric in order to reinvent it as a wholly new music and in the process reinvent the relevance of (a similarly dying) Christian faith. He was, in Heidegger's words, working at "worlding," beautifully if conservatively.

What's an example of b.? How about the Beatles's *Sgt. Pepper's,* which works within the tradition of the rock'n'roll long-playing album in order to demolish and reinvent rock'n'roll, albums and the relation-to-the-world of nearly every teenager in the Western world circa 1967.

For me, beauty is the ah! of recognition not of the sublime, or a beyond. It is the complex recognition of the complex capturing of a specific human past and the formal rerendering of that past as a whole (or, okay, as Wallace Stevens would say, parts of a whole) world. Beauty always appears as the strange within the familiar. It convinces us to desire what it desires—this strangeness—through the intensity of the pleasures its "beauty" offers. So beauty's chief anxiety is not the fear of being "ugly" but the horror of being "dead." As Dave Hicky puts it, the opposite of beauty is "the banality of neutral comfort." Beauty seduces us to desire what it desires: to be more "alive": feel this pleasure, this beauty, this strangeness. For beauty, the static quality of mere comfort is precisely despair. Needless to say, for the "socio-politically convinced," to desire to be more alive or more fully human is not necessarily to desire to be good. Thus Politic's desire to circumscribe what is tolerable in art.

My point is that we should no more wish to be done with the complicit/culpable renegade notions of art/beauty than we should wish to be done with the complicit/culpable renegade creations of sex. Simpleminded anti-essentialism and its provocative (if finally dull) companion the merely "socio-political" demand something no one should want (except end-of-history Francis Fukayama-like Republican ideologues): the termination of the human's discussion of its humanness with itself.

In the end, we are, as the painter Nicholas Africano likes to put it, "Still Human."

In spite of the facts.

1997

Marcuse and the Postmodern: A Motive for Marx

The Crisis of Marxism quickly approaches its centennial. It is surely one of the most enduring crises in the history of ideas. Nonetheless, we are not wrong to take seriously the current threats to Marx's moral and theoretical relevance. In particular, in the privileged enclaves of Western academia the spectre of postmodernism haunts not only Marxism but any form of social thought which would claim the capacity to provide a philosophical and practical project for human emancipation. Specifically, in the work of theorists like Jean Baudrillard and Jean-François Lyotard, postmodernism has taken up the analytic instruments of poststructuralism and with them revealed Marxism's incriminating "metaphysics." Marxism's critical, scientific and utopic claims have been deconstructed, and simply because they are deconstructable they have been found not to be in their final consequences different from bourgeois metaphysics. And so it is possible for Baudrillard to discover that the Marxist notion of "use value" (and the concepts of need and utility it represents) and the bourgeois notion of "exchange value" are both the product of "the mystical theology and metaphysics of bourgeois thought," are both equally a consequence of the "total mutation" underway since the dawn of bourgeois society, provided by the "ideologues of Nature." Thus, the assumption of the strategic difference between Marxist and bourgeois thought is debunked, deconstructed, and found to be a distinction without a difference.

There is a Zen expression: "At first the mountains are mountains and streams are streams. Then the mountains are not mountains and streams are not streams. But in the end, mountains are mountains again and streams are streams." If we were to apply this expression to our present situation, I think it would be easy to say that to live in the "postmodern condition" is to live in a moment where "the mountains are not mountains." Postmodernism has, in a perverse moment of philosophical gloom and glee, done away with the Real. But in the process of debunking the Real, postmodernism has also done away with the "purposefulness" of Left opposition. If there is no Real for revolution to return us to, no "true sex" (to use Michel Foucault's famous example) for a sexual revolution to revive, then what informs resistance to what we have? The challenge to contemporary Marxist thought ought to be, then, to re-arrive at a place where it is possible once again for the mountains to be mountains. That is, Marxism needs again something to serve as a motive for its activities, something to serve the purpose that the "Real" once served. The question, however, is whether this means a return of some kind to Marxism's classic certainties or a more risky and dialectical commitment to an uncertain sublation of the postmodern which might leave us one knows not where.

I would take it that postmodernism's two most serious and effective critics—Jurgen Habermas and Fredric Jameson—propose two forms of a "return" to earlier Marxist certainties. Habermas returns to the "unfinished project of modernism" and the ethical norms implicit in the Enlightenment. Jameson uses Jacques Lacan's notion of the Real to rehabilitate the fundamental historical force of the "mode of production" understood as history's "political unconscious." But few thinkers have suggested that the so-called postmodern moment is in fact not the end of history, nor a cul-de-sac from which one must return to a familiar path, but merely a moment in an ongoing dialectic. Might we dare to think that post-postmodernism could provide for us, and because of postmodernism's intervention, palpable mountains?

The purpose of this essay will be to try to suggest what might reside beyond postmodernism's horizon. But I want to make it clear from the outset that in my judgment postmodernism's truth is not something that can be simply dismissed as false. Both Habermas and Jameson seem, in Hegel's words, "fixated on the antithesis of truth and falsity." Rather, I will attend to the possibility that even postmodernism is an intellectual horizon on which the sun will eventually set, that Spirit can once again break with the world it has hitherto imagined and inhabited and submerge that world in the past. But when postmodernism is thus submerged, or, more properly, sublated, something determinate will cease, but there will also be something maintained. This is a way of saying that Marxist science, its sense of the certain, will never again be as it was. Surely, after sixty years of Western Marxism, nearly seventy years after Lukács first bravely proposed an alternative to the scientific socialism of the Third International, this is not a scandalous thing to say. In particular, postmodernism's "hermeneutics of suspicion" cannot be simply dismissed; there is in this "hermeneutics" too much of Marxism's own tradition of skepticism and critique in the face of bourgeois ideology. What I do want to propose is the idea that it is possible to imagine a yet later Marxism, flying like Hegel's owl of Minerva at dusk, for which postmodernism's radical philosophical thematics will be a new form of enabling vision.

To get to a point where one might be able to describe postmodernism's Beyond, I would like to consider in some detail the argument that Jean Baudrillard constructs in his early essay "Beyond Use Value." I choose this essay because it is representative of the work that freed Baudrillard of the influence of French Marxism in the wake of May '68. In general, work like "Beyond Use Value" established for Baudrillard his right to be indifferent to Marx while constructing his own view of the social in later texts like *Simulation, In the Shadow of the Silent Majorities, The Ecstasy of Communication,* and *America.* In the logic of Baudrillard's work as a whole, it is his early critique of Marx that serves to substantiate the assumption of his later work that Marx is irrelevant to the present. Those readers of Baudrillard familiar only with the later work must take it on faith that Baudrillard's dismissal of Marx has been elsewhere carefully done. In fact, an examination of that "dismissal" will show that there are serious problems with Baudrillard's critique. But, again, my purpose will not be to critique Baudrillard (and through him postmodernism) in order to be able to return to Marxist verities, but rather to work to the other side of the postmodern where we might hope to find, in Antonio Negri's phrase, a "Marx beyond Marx," a Marx of the next moment for which postmodernism is not merely a criminal counterrevolution run by neoconservative lackeys, but an integral part of an historical Becoming.

1

Jean Baudrillard's "Beyond Use Value" is a deconstructive critique of Marx's distinction between "use value" and "exchange value." For students of poststructuralism, the methodology is familiar. Essentially, Baudrillard has found a "binary opposition" functioning within Marx's text, a claim to a "difference" in the form of an opposition between the "natural" (use value) and the "artificial" (exchange value). Baudrillard's deconstructive strategy is then to reveal that the supposed opposition is nothing more than a "distinction without a difference." Marx's house of cards collapses.

Let's look at the steps in Baudrillard's logic.

1. Baudrillard's first assumption is that Marx's discussion of value is limited to the two terms "use value" and "exchange value." For Baudrillard, Marx maintains a radical "incomparability" between the terms. He writes: "By maintaining use value as the category of 'incomparability,' Marxist analysis has contributed to the mythology (a veritable rationalist mystique) that allows the relation of the individual to objects conceived as use values to pass for a concrete and objective—in sum, 'natural'—relation between man's needs and the function proper to the object. This is all seen as the opposite of the abstract, reified 'alienated' relation the subject would have toward products as exchange values."

2. Baudrillard then argues that the distinction between the two forms of value cannot be maintained, that use is not founded upon the natural logic of "utility," but, like exchange, is equally dependent on the logic of "equivalence." Baudrillard argues that utility is also a code, a "moral code," and is "as entirely governed by the logic of equivalence as is . . . exchange value status."

3. Marx's logic constitutes for Baudrillard an unacknowledged "fetishism of use value." Needs, like commodities, are always already fallen, are always already debased. The "need" of use value and the commodity of exchange value are the same thing.

4. Finally, for Baudrillard, "use" functions as a "providential code" under the "rubric of functionality," under the "sign of morality," "as a kind of moral law at the heart of the object." Thus, the destination of Marx's "naturalizing ideology" is the "theology of value." Marx is found out by his own critical purposes (for Baudrillard proceeds under the banner of a "critique of political economy") to be complicit with Idealism and bourgeois metaphysics.

5. In the place of Marx's vision, Baudrillard proposes a knowledge of the human in which "encompassed by objects that function and serve, man is not so much himself as the most beautiful of these functional and servile objects." He writes: "Far from the individual expressing his needs in the economic system, it is the economic system that induces the individual function and the parallel functionality of objects and needs. The individual is an ideological structure, a historical form correlative with the commodity form (exchange value) and the object form (use value). The individual is nothing but the subject thought in economic terms, rethought, simplified, and abstracted by the economy."

In the most simple terms, then, what Baudrillard has done is use deconstructive critical tools to critique Marxist economic theory. But it has also damaged Marxism's ethical ontology. It is not just the labor theory of value that is at risk here, but the sense of ethical motivation and urgency that underlines Marx's sense of the human. For in Baudrillard's critique we are presented with a structuralist version of the human in which the subject is a mere function of text (the circulation of signs), and in which the subject's sense of grievance is reduced to a mere semiotic symptom. Do not concern yourself, Baudrillard might seem to argue to a worker, with your sense that what you do is alienating, is less-than-human; your complaint is simply semiotic; in fact, since you are yourself "the most beautiful of these functional and servile objects," you have no more moral claim to a social wrong that has been perpetrated against you than does your VCR.

2

I have three general criticisms to make of Baudrillard's critique of Marx. I want first to say that Baudrillard misuses deconstruction. Second, I want to point out that Baudrillard's own thinking is far more idealist, and his later work like *Simulations* far more romantic, than anything he faults Marx for. Finally, I want to recall how much more intricate Marx's description of value is than Baudrillard allows. I want particularly to note how Marx relates his theory of value to a general philosophy of praxis. Baudrillard, I will contend, mistakes Marx's concept of use value for what Hegel would call "spurious infinity." Against Baudrillard's understanding, I will suggest that Marx's philosophy is not a philosophy of naturalized being but of historical becoming.

The idea that Baudrillard "misuses" deconstruction may seem odd; after all, deconstruction is not a methodology. However, deconstruction does have a very particular relationship to its philosophical past. For deconstruction, as for the Hegel of the *Phenomenology of Spirit,* the point of philosophy is not to demonstrate earlier philosophic positions as false in order to establish one's own position as true; rather, it is a matter of revealing that a given philosophical discourse contains its own criticism within itself. Understood in this way, Baudrillard's work, then, is clearly representative of the metaphysical tradition that deconstruction has worked to close, for Baudrillard is interested in exposing error (the error of Marxist idealism) in order better to assert his own superior Truth (the truth of the economy of signs). Baudrillard works like the vulgar ideology critic he might seem to be condemning insofar as he attempts to reveal the error of the ideological in the light of the correctness of science (semiotics; the political economy of the sign).

In effect, Baudrillard is inattentive to the deconstructive maxim that the critique is part of the problem. It is for this reason that deconstruction is not interested in others' "errors," for it is pointedly aware of its own participation in the history of that species of error we refer to as Western metaphysics. Specifically, in criticizing Marx's idealism, Baudrillard is inattentive to his own idealist constructions. For if, as I have already cited, the "economic system" induces "the individual function," and the individual is nothing but "structure," "form," and "abstraction," then Baudrillard is positing, as Kant's Copernican revolution posited, a knowledge cut off from all "external determinations" and wholly, even ecstatically, dependent on an intrinisic mesh of codes, categories and the "total circulation of signs." Baudrillard's "transcendental signifier" is signification itself. Signification is that subjective knowledge on whose noumenal "dark side," as a sort of unknowable, irretrievable objective world, are all human needs, uses and, one ought to add, injustices.

It is true that in Baudrillard's later work the apparatus of semiotics has largely fallen away, but in its place has come an equally disturbing romanticism, a nostalgia for a lost time of the Real. In the essay "Towards a Critique of the Political Economy of the Sign," this romanticism appears in the form of a desire for the "restoration of the symbolic." The symbolic is that which "haunts the sign" but about which "we can say nothing." In later texts, like *Simulations,* Baudrillard thinks even more grossly of a lost "real": "It is no longer a question of imitation, nor of reduplication, nor even of parody. It is rather a question of substituting signs of the real for the real itself, that is, an operation to deter every real process by its operational double, a metastable, programmatic, perfect descriptive machine which provides all the signs of the real and short-circuits all its vicissitudes."

Baudrillard even argues in the mode that he had criticized Marx for in "Beyond Use Value"; he suggests a radical opposition between "human goals" and the "law of equivalence," and he goes so far as to imply that capital is responsible for this—what other word is there for it?—alienation: "For, finally, it was capital which was the first to feed throughout its history on the destruction of every referential, of every human goal, which shattered every ideal distinction between true and false, good and evil, in order to establish a radical law of equivalence and exchange, the iron law of its power." Clearly, Baudrillard is asserting that the strategy of the capitalist system is to generate this abstract structure of signification which has as a consequence the total commodification of all human experience. Baudrillard's curious argument is not, as Derrida would surely insist, that the real is textual and always has been, but that the real has "disappeared" and been replaced by capitalist simulation. To be sure, Baudrillard is clear in maintaining that there is no return to the real, and that the "ecstasy of communication" is our certain fate, but he does not deny the real as a historical premise. This makes of his thought an occulted philosophy of the authentic. The world of simulation is miserable not because the real is and always was a simulacrum (a more consistent position for him to take) but because in the world of simulation we are still aware of having lost the real, of having fallen from it.

Finally, the most serious lapse in Baudrillard's critique of Marx is his separation of Marx's discussion of value from its proper place in Marx's more general philosophy of praxis. Baudrillard's strategy seems to be to insist that "use value" be understood as a natural given, as a metaphysical presence. He means to turn it into being. Were this Marx's intent, he would be guilty of positing what Hegel calls "spurious infinity." In the *Science of Logic* Hegel tries to distinguish his conception of the infinite from Kant's. In Kant the infinite is posited over against the finite in a relation wherein they are "qualitatively distinct others." Thus, the infinite of Kant's Understanding stands against the merely finite phenomenal reality of sensuous intuition. To think through the problem as Baudrillard encourages us, we might imagine that the growing of wheat or the baking of a loaf of bread stands as finite against the infinity of "Use Value" as a Marxian transcendental category. The radical distinctness of infinite and finite in Kant is what Hegel calls "spurious infinity." On the other hand, Hegel's development of the infinite is "a return from the empty flight" of Kant's Understanding. In Hegel, the infinite is neither an aloof absolute difference, nor mere unity of finite and infinite; the true infinite "is essentially only as a becoming." What Baudrillard's analysis of Marx's notion of production occludes (in both *For a Critique of the Political Economy of the Sign* and *The Mirror of Production*) is the intimate relationship of Marx's concept of production to Marx's general philosophical anthropology of praxis, a philosophy with profound debts to Hegel. Baudrillard wants simply to maintain that for Marx there is an a priori human need—hunger—which is answered by production—the making of bread—resulting in value, the usefulness of the bread. But this is a travesty of Marx's thinking on the subject of production and value.

It is a fundamental theme of "The Economic and Philosophic Manuscripts of 1844" that production is not simply a matter of economics, industry and providing for basic needs; production is first, for Marx, the historical project of the human, of the social construction of needs. When the human is alienated from its productive capacities, it is a social alienation from the social authority over the invention and development of needs within human communities. In the place of this social autonomy comes a minimal understanding of need, set by the capitalist: the need to sustain the worker as labor power, that is, to provide the minimal requirements of food and shelter in order to reproduce labor power on a daily basis. What Baudrillard has in mind as the be-all of production in use value, Marx would call merely "animal"; Baudrillard's understanding of use value is limited to the capitalist's understanding of use value, the bare necessities for reproducing labor power: "Certainly eating, drinking, procreating, etc., are also genuinely human functions. But in the abstraction which separates them from the sphere of all other human activity and turns them into sole and ultimate ends, they are animal."

It is this "sphere of all other human activity" with which Baudrillard is peculiarly unconcerned. But Marx himself is precisely concerned with this "sphere," for it is this sphere which takes his thinking beyond the simple notion of industrial production to which Baudrillard would like to limit Marx. Marx writes:

> For in the first place labour, life-activity, productive life itself, appears to man merely as a means of satisfying a need—the need to maintain the physical existence. Yet the productive life is the life of the species. It is life-engendering life. The whole character of a species—its species character—is contained in the character of its life-activity; and free, conscious activity is man's species character. Life itself appears only as a means to life . . . The object of labour is, therefore, the objectification of man's species life: for he duplicates himself not only, as in consciousness, intellectually, but also actively, in reality, and therefore he contem-

plates himself in a world that he has created.

For Marx there is no notion of an essential human nature, with needs already set forth (unless one wanted to argue that it is human nature to create its nature). Rather, the human is committed concretely and historically to the summoning of its nature through its sensuous activities. Marx understands that human production is not the mere animal fulfillment of need through eating; the human is precisely the always-already-in-process construction of a world for eating: cuisine. As Hegel wrote, and Marx cannot have failed to observe, "human nature only really exists in an achieved community of minds."

It is possible that this "achieved community" is susceptible to semiotic description. It is possible that, as Baudrillard anticipates, the social can be articulated through codes, mechanisms, and systems of signs. But the semiotic arrangement of culture must not be understood as an absolute background, for that would make it impossible to say how and why culture changes, and, more importantly, why it ought to change. In order to begin to explain such shifts one needs a theory of culture as the scene of a struggle over the social authority to determine what will count as need, right, content, etc. Baudrillard's totalized semiotic vision leaves little room for this heteroglot understanding of culture as the scene of a struggle over the right to create need.

When Baudrillard reduces Marx's notion of production to the simplistic idea of "natural need," and uses this "idealist flaw" to boot Marx from the field (Baudrillard's *Forget Foucault* was just a postscript to his older project to "forget Marx"), he is working to eliminate the possibility of a cogent social antagonism. In the place of antagonism, Baudrillard has provided a kind of erotics or euphorics of bondage within the network of cultural (especially "pop" cultural) signification. America, in particular, is an appeal to the idea that political resistance isn't sexy, is passé, is something only for ludicrous-seeming "Californian scholars with monomaniacal passions for things French or Marxist," and that we have no alternatives to a kind of langorous, passive capitulation to the flow, the circulation of money, power, but primarily signs through our bodies:

Ravishing hyperrealism
Ecstatic asceticism
Multi-process tracking shot
Interactive multi-dimensionality
Mind-blowing

In effect, Baudrillard's construction of history is a simple morality play in which the Real has been "ravished," and we must now suffer infinitely the consequences of that ravishing: life in the "hyperreal" (that is to say, life in a cultural context devoid of a role for the Real; life in a context of pure simulation).

But even if one grants Baudrillard's claim that we reside in the hyperreal, hyperrealism's present historical moment is not necessarily a moment of irredeemable "damage." The postmodern moment, like earlier historical moments, is also "restive" because it contains the possibility and perhaps even the tendency to liberate the social from any entrenched understanding of how social reality ought to be. Never before has capitalism's ideological hold on the nature of the Real been so evidently frail. Certainly, every teenage computer hacker, and probably every teenager, who has grown up not so much absurd as mutant, their social genetics bombarded from day one by video, computers, fractal reality, the Simulated at its most Sublime (both terrifying and intoxicating), all of these citizens of the future know that reality is up for grabs. This is a potential, a tendency in the present moment that those with an emancipatory vision, those who want to maintain modernity's project for the realization of human possibility, ought to place in it both hope and energy. What we ought to be contesting in the postmodern moment is not so much cyber-reality itself, but techno-capitalism's strategy for appropriating that reality for the more old-fashioned purpose of domination abroad and repression at home. In short, capitalism's sin against the human has been and remains its tendency to make the world "one dimensional."

3

It should be clear by this point that the logic of political resistance I am attempting to develop has two principal components. The first is a commitment to reexamining and re-appropriating the fundamentals of Marxist-Hegelian philosophical anthropology as an ethical and ontological motivation for resistance. The second is an insistence that it will not do to pretend that the so-called "postmodern condition" as a historical and theoretical moment is something that can simply be rejected as false in order to return to older socialist truths. In the last section of this paper, I would like to show that the thought of Herbert Marcuse, especially the thinking in *Reason and Revolution* and *Eros and Civilization,* is one of the richest grounds for showing how the synthesis of Marx-Hegel and postmodernism might be accomplished. Obviously, such a synthesis will not get us "beyond" postmodernism in any absolute sense. However, it is important to see that the logic of postmodernism does not require the defeat of what Hegel called the Concept: Freedom. Marcuse can help us to see how the Concept not only survives the withering interrogations of postmodernism but is strengthened by its insights.

Marcuse's work of the '40s and '50s is striking for two reasons. First, this work is remarkable for its understanding of Hegel and its contentions for Hegel's enduring relevance to political thought. Until Lukács's work on the "young Hegel," and Alexandre Kojev's and Jean Hyppolite's seminars were translated into English, Marcuse's book was virtually the only source for a materialist understanding of what it was in Hegel that inspired Marx. Second, we can see in Marcuse's work of this period many of the most important themes of postmodernism. I would like to call attention to two "postmodern" themes which have striking resonances within Marcuse's work: the concept of repressive "performativity" and the concept of liberatory "free play."

The concept of performativity is central to Jean-François Lyotard's book *The Post-modern Condition.* In that work, Lyotard uses the idea of performativity to describe a situation in which the dominant social forces are no longer required to legitimate their interests ideologically through the use of "meta-narratives" because the "grand narratives" have lost their credibility. In the place of ideological legitimation comes the pure appeal of maximizing functional efficiency:

> The State and/or company must abandon the idealist and humanist narratives of legitimation in order to justify the new goal: in the discourse of today's financial backers of research, the only credible goal is power. . . . [I]n post-industrial societies the normativity of laws is replaced by the performativity of procedures. "Context control," in other words, performance improvement won at the expense of the partner or partners constituting that context (be they "nature" or men), can pass for a kind of legitimation. De facto legitimation.

As a consequence: "Research sectors that are unable to argue that they contribute even indirectly to the optimization of the system's performance are abandoned by the flow of capital and doomed to senescence. The criterion of performance is explicitly invoked by the authorities to justify their refusal to subsidize certain research centers." Lyotard's notion of "performativity" is very similar to Marcuse's concept of the "performance principle." Marcuse argues that the performance principle works in Western bourgeois culture not because of any rational relation to human need or desire, but because, says Marcuse, quoting P. W. Bridgman, we "no longer permit ourselves to use as tools in our thinking concepts of which we cannot give an adequate account in terms of operations": "Bridgman's prediction has come true. The new mode of thought (operationalism) is today the predominant tendency in philosophy, psychology, sociology, and other fields. Many of the most seriously troublesome concepts are being "eliminated" by showing that no adequate account of them in terms of operations or behavior can be given.

The enormous difference between Lyotard and Marcuse resides in the fact that Lyotard sees performativity as the ineluctable consequence of our "condition," against which there are no possible appeals because of the postmodern conviction that such an appeal would require the construction of a "master narrative." Marcuse, on

1 1 3

the other hand, less frightened of the seductions of master narratives (Marxist or otherwise), sees this condition as an injury, as the "apex of alienation": "To say that the job must be done because it is a 'job' is truly the apex of alienation, the total loss of instinctual and intellectual freedom—repression which has become, not the second, but the first nature of man." Here, in a society dominated by the principle of performativity, the dialectic of becoming, of the realization of human potential, is halted by what Marcuse calls in *Reason and Revolution* "a reality in which all logic and all speech are false to the extent that they are part of a mutilated whole." This reality has been brought about by that version of Reason which functions as technical domination. This much Lyotard would have little difficulty in assenting to. But Marcuse goes further in arguing that "Reason, and Reason alone, contains its own corrective." Insofar as Reason is the origin of the opposite of its original promise (it has provided domination rather than liberation), it has created a situation of self-contradiction. Here Marcuse is most Hegelian and least like the postmodernists, for he argues that, "the presence of the contradiction makes man restive; he struggles to overcome his given external state. The contradiction thus has the force of an 'Ought' that impels him to realize that which does not as yet exist." However, this difference should not be taken to mean that postmodernism's descriptions of the present moment are therefore wrong. Rather, what Marcuse's example suggests is that the defeatism and political quietism of recent postmodern thought is not an unavoidable part of its accounts of the present historical moment. If it means anything to describe something called postmodernism, it is not because it is a qualitatively different animal altogether. Postmodernism is the extension and the intensification of tendencies which one can find in thinking which preceded it. Postmodern theorists like Baudrillard and Lyotard are indebted to the achievements of the ideology criticism of the Frankfurt School, and Marxist structuralists like Louis Althusser and Roland Barthes, a debt that they acquired in the Marxist milieu of pre-'68 Paris. But postmodernism is unlike its predecessors in the nearly total absence of ethical content in its diagnosis of techno-capitalism. Largely because of its simplistic commitment to the poststructural critique of metaphysics and master narratives, postmodernism is not willing to entertain the possibility that our present techno-totalization is a form of damage, that it is something that we ought to resent, or that there are imaginable social forms which we might legitimately prefer to it. The present is simply our "mode," perhaps our final mode. However, there is one postmodern "theme," again one imagined in considerable detail by Marcuse, which could correct this ethical lack: the theme of "play." Marcuse's use of the idea of play is most conspicuous in his book on Freud, *Eros and Civilization,* where he speaks of "the free play of the released potentialities of man and nature." Nonetheless, my contention would be that the origin of Marcuse's use of "play" is not in Freud but in his brilliant understanding of Hegel's philosophy of becoming. For Marcuse, Hegel's philosophy is not merely about the "restiveness" of an Ought that impels the human "to realize that which does not as yet exist" and which eventually culminates in the static reality of the Absolute. Rather, Marcuse's understanding of Hegel shows that the Absolute itself is "restive" or "dynamic." As Marcuse argues in the chapter "Philosophical Interlude" in *Eros and Civilization:*

> the highest form of reason is, to Hegel, almost the opposite of the prevailing form: it is attained and sustained fulfillment, the transparent unity of subject and object, of the universal and the individual—a dynamic rather than static unity in which all becoming is free self-externalization *(Entausserung),* release and "enjoyment" of potentialities.

To be sure, Marcuse understands that the Absolute is different from the history which preceded it. Whatever dynamism it contains is not the dynamism of "supercession," of the sublation of one historical moment by another. The Absolute cannot be about this form of transcendence because it is by definition the end of history insofar as, in the space of the Absolute, Freedom is at last realized. But for Marcuse the content of Freedom is not static. What will make the Absolute dynamic, unlike the history which led to it, will be not the despair of unrealized Spirit but the absolute openness of human possibility, which would be the presentation of an infinite horizon of never fully realizable potential. Within Marcuse's profound illumination of Hegel, "Being is continuous becoming." Through

Marcuse's unique understanding of the Absolute he assists Hegel to achieve Hegel's original ambition, expressed in the Phenomenology of Spirit, "to think pure change." However, in contrast to the "spurious infinity" discussed above, Marcuse maintains that Hegel's Infinite "had to result from a stricter interpretation of finitude." Marcuse continues:

> As a matter of fact, we find that the analysis of objective things has already taken us from the finite to the infinite. For the process in which a finite thing perishes and, in perishing, becomes another finite thing, which repeats the same, is in itself a process ad infinitum, and not only in the superficial sense that the progression cannot be broken. When a finite thing "perishes into" another thing, it has changed itself, inasmuch as perishing is its way of consummating its true potentialities. The incessant perishing of things is thus an equally continuous negation of their finitude. It is infinity.

For Marcuse, Hegel's Absolute is a place for inspired and human Play. If there is anything static about Marcuse's notion of Hegel's Absolute, it has lost its repressive connotations. It is "the order of gratification." In the Absolute, "static triumphs over dynamic; but it is a static that moves in its own fullness—a productivity that is sensuousness, play, and song."

Oddly enough, the postmodern thinkers who come closest to Marcuse's understanding of the Absolute as free play, free development of human possibility, are Gilles Deleuze and Felix Guattari in whose concept of "Nomadology" the emancipatory potential of the postmodern emerges in a provocative philosophical rendering of human creativity. I say this is odd because Deleuze and Guattari have made a point of identifying Hegel as everything their own thought is not about. However, it is quite clear that the Hegel they object to is the "Hegel of the Right" that "weds the destiny of thought to the State." On the other hand, Marcuse's Hegel, the Hegel of the *Phenomenology of Spirit* and the *Science of Logic,* would seem to be very much in sympathy with Deleuze and

Guattari's critique of the static "striated space" of the State. As Marcuse wisely observes in *Reason and Revolution,* "the historical heritage of Hegel's philosophy did not pass to the Hegelians." Rather, "the history of Hegelianism became the history of a struggle against Hegel in which he was used as a symbol for all that the new intellectual . . . efforts opposed." Deleuze and Guattari may be part of this secret history of Hegelianism. For Marcuse, Hegel's Spirit is very much what Deleuze and Guattari call a "war machine"; it is the idea which negates the negation of the State or the present Reality. One might very well say of Marcuse's understanding of Hegelian Spirit what Deleuze and Guattari say in *A Thousand Plateaus* of the War Machine: "It is at the moment the war machine ceases to exist, conquered by the State, that it displays to the utmost its irreducibility, that it scatters into thinking, loving, dying, or creating machines which have at their disposal vital or revolutionary powers capable of challenging the conquering State." The emancipatory appeal of "play" resides in its world-making potential. It is a form of radical democracy based upon a radical philosophy of becoming over a static philosophy of being, of difference over presence, of an ad infinitum "worlding" over Nature, of infinite Nomadological "lines of flight" over the striated space of the political State. "Play" is both the irruption of a metamorphic emancipation and the utopic power of a "pure and immeasurable multiplicity." Thus, a certain liberatory logic begins to appear within the postmodern project (not "condition"), a logic that I think both Marcuse and at least one version of Hegel would find inspiring. If the real is constituted not by simple presence (Hegel's "sense certainty"; Lukács's "positivity") but by "difference," by the activity of texts, commodities and the world of signs; and if the possibilities for how those worlds are constituted are without necessary limit; then, a political economy which "mutilates artisans in order to make 'workers' of them" (Deleuze and Guattari), which reifies the world through commodities, and which compels social conformity either through the bourgeois ideologemes of Nature or the obligations of the performance principle, this political economy is a form of social injury. If the logic of signs allows for "worlding" without limit, let these worlds begin. It is our sense of the truth of the unlimited possibilities of the social that provokes our outrage when colonialism, neocolonialism, or what Paul Virilio calls endocolonialism, seeks to foreclose on cultural difference, to homogenize the more and more sinister-seeming "global village." So, if there is an ecstasy in the semiotic understanding of the real as a place defined not by the presence of things but by a difference constituted by signs, it is not to be found in the ecstasy of Baudrillard's sad conductors of information, it is in Derrida's appeal to us "to speak, to make our voices resonate throughout the corridors in order to make up for the breakup of presence." This "resonance," the play of our voices in the labyrinth of that text we refer to as the world, holds the potential for a kind of value, even a human value, that we have not yet learned how to claim.

Needless to say, such an ethical strand in the postmodern project does not provide for a complete ethics. Enormous theoretical issues remain, not least of which is the status of the "individual" and the relevance of "agency" in all of this. But I believe that Marcuse's illumination of Hegel allows for a negation of the negation of mere alterity so that, to recall the Zen maxim with which I began, the "mountains can be mountains" again. No doubt we will not all prefer these mountains, distinctly diminished from their former romantic grandeur and made dependent on the "resonance of voice." One hundred-and-fifty years after Hegel, we are still not comfortable with the idea that nature is something that is generated within historical human communities. However, it is important to see that through Hegel's philosophy of becoming, generating both Marcuse's and postmodernism's celebration of play, an essential social attribute is salvaged from the wreck of Western metaphysics. Hegel's revelation, pursued so purposefully by Marx and Marcuse after him, has provided mountains and a world that are truly ours. We need to reclaim that world so that we might present it with hope to the future. And certainly the fact that the world is not something given to us by God, Nature, the State, or even the logic of signs, but rather something created by ourselves concretely and historically, this should not make us care about such a world any less. Perhaps if we come to know the world in this way, we will be all the more ashamed of how little we have made of it.

1992

118

Curtis White,

born in 1951, is the author of *Heretical Songs* (1951),

Metaphysics in the Midwest (1988),

The Idea of Home (1992),

Anarcho-Hindu (1995),

and *Memories of My Father Watching TV* (1998).

DALKEY ARCHIVE PAPERBACKS

FELIPE ALFAU, *Chromos.*
Locos.
Sentimental Songs.
ALAN ANSEN,
Contact Highs: Selected Poems 1957-1987.
DJUNA BARNES, *Ladies Almanack.*
Ryder.
JOHN BARTH, *LETTERS.*
Sabbatical.
ANDREI BITOV, *Pushkin House.*
ROGER BOYLAN, *Killoyle.*
CHRISTINE BROOKE-ROSE, *Amalgamemnon.*
GERALD BURNS, *Shorter Poems.*
MICHEL BUTOR,
Portrait of the Artist as a Young Ape.
JULIETA CAMPOS, *The Fear of Losing Eurydice.*
ANNE CARSON, *Eros the Bittersweet.*
LOUIS-FERDINAND CÉLINE, *Castle to Castle.*
North.
Rigadoon.
HUGO CHARTERIS, *The Tide Is Right.*
JEROME CHARYN, *The Tar Baby.*
EMILY HOLMES COLEMAN, *The Shutter of Snow.*
ROBERT COOVER, *A Night at the Movies.*
STANLEY CRAWFORD,
Some Instructions to My Wife.
RENÉ CREVEL, *Putting My Foot in It.*
RALPH CUSACK, *Cadenza.*
SUSAN DAITCH, *Storytown.*
PETER DIMOCK,
A Short Rhetoric for Leaving the Family.
COLEMAN DOWELL, *Island People.*
Too Much Flesh and Jabez.
RIKKI DUCORNET, *The Fountains of Neptune.*
The Jade Cabinet.
Phosphor in Dreamland.
The Stain.

WILLIAM EASTLAKE, *Lyric of the Circle Heart.*
STANLEY ELKIN, *The Dick Gibson Show.*
ANNIE ERNAUX, *Cleaned Out.*
LAUREN FAIRBANKS, *Muzzle Thyself.*
Sister Carrie.
LESLIE A. FIEDLER,
Love and Death in the American Novel.
RONALD FIRBANK, *Complete Short Stories.*
FORD MADOX FORD, *The March of Literature.*
JANICE GALLOWAY, *Foreign Parts.*
The Trick Is to Keep Breathing.
WILLIAM H. GASS,
Willie Masters' Lonesome Wife.
C. S. GISCOMBE, *Giscome Road.*
Here.
KAREN ELIZABETH GORDON, *The Red Shoes.*
GEOFFREY GREEN, ET AL, *The Vineland Papers.*
PATRICK GRAINVILLE, *The Cave of Heaven.*
JOHN HAWKES, *Whistlejacket.*
ALDOUS HUXLEY, *Antic Hay.*
Point Counter Point.
Those Barren Leaves.
Time Must Have a Stop.
TADEUSZ KONWICKI, *The Polish Complex.*
EWA KURYLUK, *Century 21.*
OSMAN LINS,
The Queen of the Prisons of Greece.
ALF MAC LOCHLAINN,
The Corpus in the Library.
Out of Focus.
D. KEITH MANO, *Take Five.*
BEN MARCUS, *The Age of Wire and String.*
DAVID MARKSON, *Collected Poems.*
Reader's Block.
Springer's Progress.
Wittgenstein's Mistress.
CARL R. MARTIN, *Genii Over Salzburg.*

Visit our website at www.cas.ilstu.edu/english/dalkey/dalkey.html